Christianity and the Ancient Mysteries

Reflections on Rudolf Steiner's *Christianity as Mystical Fact*

Charles Kovacs

Floris
Books

First published in 2017 by Floris Books

© 2017 Estate of Charles Kovacs

British Library CIP data available
ISBN 978-178250-447-4
Printed in Great Britain by TJ International

Christianity and the Ancient Mysteries

Contents

Foreword

Charles Kovacs was a class teacher at the Edinburgh Rudolf Steiner School for many years. Several of his working notes for the main lesson subjects given in Waldorf schools have already been published by Floris Books and are now well known in educational circles. But during his time as a teacher, and for many years afterwards, Kovacs also gave lectures and held regular study groups. The present volume contains his own notes for a series of twenty-five such group meetings based around a study of Rudolf Steiner's book *Christianity as Mystical Fact*. Making careful notes was part of Kovacs' preparation method, but he never used any notes during the actual meetings, preferring to speak freely on the subject.

Although accessible to any interested reader, the work he left to us reflects a lifetime of experience and study. While dealing straightforwardly with spiritual themes it is also very relevant to some of the intractable questions affecting the modern world.

Though they were not part of the original manuscript, references have been added for those who like to follow things up for themselves in the anthroposophical literature.

Throughout his busy life Charles Kovacs also devoted as much time as he could to painting and drawing. A few examples of his paintings are included in the present volume.

Howard Copland, 2017

The chapters in *Christianity as Mystical Fact*

1972 UK edition	2008 US edition	Chapters in this book
1. Points of View	(in Appendix)	
2. The Mysteries and their Wisdom	1. The Mysteries and Mysteriosophy	1–2
3. Greek Sages before Plato	2. Mysteries and Pre-Socratic Philosophy	3
4. Plato as a Mystic	3. Platonic Mysteries	4
5. Wisdom of the Mysteries and Myth	4. Myth and Mysteriosophy	5–10
6. Egyptian Mystery Wisdom	5. Egyptian and Other Eastern Mysteries	11–12
7. The Gospels	6. The Evidence of Gospels	13
8. The Lazarus Miracle	7. The 'Miracle' of Lazarus	14
9. The Apocalypse of John	8. The Apocalypse of John	15–18
10. Jesus and His Historical Background	9. Jesus in His Historical Setting	19
11. The Nature of Christianity	10. The Essence of Christianity	20–23
12. Christianity and Pagan Wisdom	11. Christian and Pagan Wisdom	24
13. Augustine and the Church	12. Augustine and the Church	25

1

The Secrecy of the Mysteries

Mystics after Modernism and *Christianity as Mystical Fact* are the first books by Rudolf Steiner which could be called anthroposophical. All his previous works were philosophical. These two books, which herald the coming of spiritual science or anthroposophy, contain as yet none of the later terminology (astral body, etheric body, etc.), nor is there any mention of the author's own clairvoyant research. Yet we can be sure that – especially in *Christianity as Mystical Fact* – Steiner's spiritual knowledge stood behind his statements. This applies in particular to his description of the ancient mystery temples and their function. It is a subject about which history has little to say, simply because very little can be known from documents, which are the historian's only source. Rudolf Steiner uses only what can be gleaned from the works of historians but infuses the dry historical facts with an insight which stems from a higher knowledge than can be found in mere scholarship.

The reason why there is such a paucity of tangible information about the mystery temples is not difficult to discern. No one was admitted to the mysteries without having first sworn a sacred oath not to reveal to outsiders anything revealed in the temple. The penalty for any breach of secrecy was death. Nothing can illustrate better the seriousness of this threat than the case of the Greek playwright Aeschylus. He was charged with having revealed a mystery secret in one of his plays and he fled to the altar of Dionysus, which was regarded as an asylum, a sacred precinct from which no one could be taken by force.

While under the protection of this sanctuary, Aeschylus offered to stand trial before an Athenian court which would decide whether or not he deserved death. The offer was accepted and Aeschylus proved at the trial that he had never been admitted to any mystery temple and so could not betray any mystery secrets. Whatever it was in the play that aroused the avenging fury of the mystery guardians was only the product of his own mind.

The secrecy surrounding the mysteries was not an arbitrary law invented by men intending to keep certain kinds of knowledge among themselves. The rule of secrecy, handed down from generation to generation, originated in the spiritual world. As Steiner explained in a later chapter of *Christianity as Mystical Fact,* Jesus broke this rule when he performed an initiation ritual at the so-called 'raising' of Lazarus. Perhaps he too could have pleaded that he had not been admitted to any mystery cults; but he did not plead at all or seek protection in a sanctuary. And so, whatever other reasons were given for the death sentence and the crucifixion it was, according to this book, the raising of Lazarus which constituted a most serious breach of mystery secrets and which demanded the death penalty. But at the crucifixion the veil before the Holy of Holies in the temple was rent in two: a sign that the mysteries and the law of secrecy had come to an end. The spiritual world itself spoke in this event of the rending of the veil.

But even when secrecy was still the law, certain mystery matters were permitted to be revealed. There was, for instance, the Roman author Apuleius, who lived in the third century AD and who was an initiate of the Isis mysteries which had by that time spread from Egypt to Rome. Apuleius wrote a book called *The Golden Ass* which is a curious mixture – partly a bawdy story of witchcraft and depravity in decadent Rome and partly a profound mystical allegory in the tale of Eros and Psyche – but which contains at the end a description of the author's own initiation experience. It is in such general terms that it could not have meant much to outsiders but conveys a great deal to anyone acquainted with Rudolf Steiner's initiation knowledge.

Apuleius writes:

> I approached the underworld even to the gates of
> Proserpina.
> I was dispersed in all the elements.
> I saw the upper gods and the lower gods and
> worshipped them
> And I saw the sun at midnight.

The 'underworld' and the 'gates of Proserpina' are called in modern terminology the 'threshold' and what Apuleius experienced is the 'crossing of the threshold'. The 'elements' are an experience of the etheric forces. The upper gods and the lower gods are the beings who endow man with the soul-forces of thinking on the one side and willing on the other. The 'sun at midnight' is an actual clairvoyant observation but it also indicates a certain stage of development: to be conscious when one is in the condition of sleep, with the I and astral body outside the physical and etheric bodies.[1] The 'sun' is both what is seen and what makes consciousness in the sleep condition possible.

Our normal waking consciousness is the result of the sense-impressions which comprise the physical world and the physical body. When in brain-washing experiments the sense-impressions are to a large extent eliminated, human consciousness is dimmed to a kind of half-awake stupor. In the ancient mysteries to which Apuleius belonged, the strength to remain awake outside the body, without sense-impressions, was provided by the priests who enacted the ritual of initiation. It was *their* spiritual strength which gave the neophyte the inner light, the inner sun to 'see' without physical eyes. And what distinguished higher beings, the gods, from man was the power of self-sustaining consciousness, a consciousness that exists through its own strength. And this brings us to another witness from antiquity, one quoted by Rudolf Steiner in this chapter, Plutarch, the Greek historian.

According to this writer, the initiate greets the god with the words, 'Thou art.' It would be a meaningless formula if it only stated that the god exists as trees or animals or men exist. But the god's existence is a *deed,* his own deed. It is not bestowed on him as it is on mortal man. There is an experience one can have quite often with young children, which touches this mystery of divine existence. One tells a child that the world and all there is in it was made by God. Sometimes the child will ask, 'But who made God?' And the adult can only answer, 'No one else made God, he made himself.' When we give such an answer we are not aware of what it means. But the initiate who, in Plutarch's account, meets a divine being experiences the full impact of encountering an entity who *is,* who *exists,* through itself, by its own power and as its own deed. This is meant by the words, 'Thou art.'

But these words lead us to another utterance, one which is spoken by a god to man. The Old Testament speaks of this encounter in the form of an imagination; the story should not be regarded as a physical event. What we are told in this story is that Moses encountered a burning bush which was not consumed by the fire. A god speaks to him from the flames and commands him to lead the Israelites out of Egypt. And when Moses answers that they will want to know the name of the god who gave this command, the god in the flames speaks, 'I am the I am.'

Here again the verb 'to be' is not to be understood as referring to existence *given* to a being. 'I am through my own being, through the "I am"': this is proclaimed by the voice from the flames. And with these words begins an evolution which leads to another voice that said, 'I am the Way, the Truth and the Life' – or, as we now have to understand it: 'The I am is the Way, the Truth and the Life.'[2]

For Plutarch, as for Apuleius, consciousness during the initiation sleep was maintained by the spiritual forces of the priests. And meeting a divine, self-sustaining consciousness he could only say 'Thou art.' For Moses it was a god who said 'I am' but this too was a divinity outside the human soul.

It was only the Mystery of Golgotha which brought to humanity the possibility of finding the 'I am' within the soul – which means a consciousness awake through its own strength; independent of sense-perception, independent of the physical body. Through the Mystery of Golgotha the 'I am' of the gods has been given to mankind. This is the reason why, in the mysteries of our time, it cannot be officiating priests who give strength to one's consciousness but only one's own 'I am.' By quoting Plutarch's 'Thou art' Rudolf Steiner gave the broad outline of the whole book and, in a sense, of his own task: to lay the foundation of the new mysteries, the mysteries of the 'I am'.

Once it is understood that the time for the new mysteries has come, the references to the ancient mysteries in this book, as well as in many other works by Rudolf Steiner, acquire a significance well beyond mere historical interest. In the course of the millennia in which there were mystery temples, many thousands of people found admittance and reached some lower or higher degree of initiation. What did it mean to these souls that they had gone through supersensible experiences, what did it mean to them in their subsequent incarnations? Rudolf Steiner said of Leonardo da Vinci that he had once been an initiate of the mysteries,[3] one can see from this example that initiation experiences create faculties in later incarnations.

But there is also something else which does not apply to Leonardo, because he was born in the Kali Yuga, the Dark Age, which does apply to our time. Ever since 1899 when the Kali Yuga came to an end, there was a current which ran against the dominant materialistic tendencies. It sometimes produced strange and grotesque phenomena – from the theosophists to the believers in flying saucers, from the re-emergence of astrology as a thriving industry to acupuncture – from faith-healing to witches' covens. The list of attempts to reach an 'alternative' understanding of man and the world is endless. And all these attempts are symptoms of a thirst for spiritual knowledge which, in as far as it existed at all in the nineteenth century, was limited to small secretive groups. Out of this broad twentieth-century stream a relatively small number of souls were attracted by Rudolf Steiner's anthroposophy. What was the attraction? Not sober evaluation, not conscious rational judgement, but a kind of instinctive recognition. It is as if one had heard this kind of thing before. And one really has – in one of the ancient mystery schools. And when Rudolf Steiner speaks of these pre-Christian mysteries, as he does in so many of his works, it is as if he were saying 'Don't you remember?'

The souls who feel a deep genuine connection with anthroposophy (which is not the same as being a member of the Anthroposophical Society) are those who have met anthroposophy in quite other forms before – in the ancient mystery centres. And what we can learn about them through Rudolf Steiner's books is something of our own past, our own spiritual biography.

2

Mystery Knowledge and Popular Religion

Towards the end of the chapter 'Mysteries and Mystery Wisdom' Rudolf Steiner draws attention to the relationship between the mysteries and the religious beliefs of the outside world. This relationship is of the utmost importance for an understanding of the following chapters and therefore needs special consideration.

Those who had found admittance to the mysteries were in no doubt that the gods of the popular religions resembled human beings in so many ways that the conclusion was inescapable: these gods are the creation of the human mind. It was a conclusion which, in a much later period of history, in the nineteenth century, led the German philosopher Ludwig Feuerbach (a convinced atheist) to state, 'It is not God who created man in his image but man who created God in his image.' Yet for the pupils of the mysteries the recognition of the human origin of the popular mythologies did not lead to a rejection of religion or to atheism. The reason why the mystery wisdom was not in opposition to popular religion is given by Rudolf Steiner in a remarkable statement to the effect that the mysteries understood how popular mythologies had come about: the divine creative forces at work in nature also work in man and create, in him, the images of the gods.

It is a remarkable statement because it describes a situation which does not exist today – the dreamlike imaginations which were still 'natural' in ancient times. They were natural

15

in the same way as the growth of a plant is natural. And the mysteries provided a way to go beyond the imaginations to the divine forces which were behind the imaginations as they were behind the growth of plants.

This understanding of the real origin of the various mythologies was not available to the nineteenth-century philosopher; he could only draw the atheist conclusion. But we can also see from the true insight of the ancient mysteries why Rudolf Steiner referred so often in his work to one or another of these mythologies, why he pointed out again and again the spiritual truth and profound wisdom contained in myths, sagas and legends. And, in doing so, he makes us aware that the task of our time is to come to conscious imaginations, to images which are our own deed as the images of the past were deeds of the gods.

The mysteries wanted to lead human souls to the beings and forces which are 'behind' nature as they are 'behind' the mythologies. They could say to their pupils, 'the real gods are hidden in the imaginations of mythology – they are hidden in your own souls and it is this hidden divine reality within yourself which you have to find.'

In order to come nearer to this mystery of the hidden God, Rudolf Steiner introduces here a word which is itself pure mythology, he uses the term 'enchanted'. God is enchanted in the world around us, he is enchanted within us. This is more than a somewhat poetic image for the hidden presence of God. It is a word which should provoke the question: who could cast a spell on God, who could be the sorcerer powerful enough to make the Almighty a powerless enchanted presence, unable to reveal himself? And the answer is, no one but God himself. And here Rudolf Steiner approaches what is unquestionably the most profound of all mysteries.

It can help us to understand this mystery if we consider the simple act of seeing. The organ by means of which we see the world around us is the eye. But we could not see at all if, in the act of seeing, the eye would draw attention to itself. It does not.

It is quite 'selfless' and through this selflessness of the eye our own soul-life is enriched by the visible world. If God were to make his immediate presence felt, the soul could, before his splendour, not be aware of anything else, not of the world, nor of its own existence.

And there *is* a myth – how could it be otherwise – which hints at this mystery. Zeus had taken a human form to become the lover of Semele, a king's daughter. Jealous Hera, the goddess-wife of Zeus, disguised as an old woman, persuaded her to insist that her lover should show himself in his true nature. Eventually Zeus did so – and Semele was consumed by the fire of a bolt of lightning. The human soul could not bear the immediate experience of divinity – it would be annihilated by it. And it is God's love for the human soul which is the reason for the 'enchantment' – for the disguise – for his being hidden.

It is so not only for us human beings but even for beings of a much higher order. They too could not exist, they too would be consumed by the direct experience of God as himself. All that exists in the world owes this existence to God not asserting *his* existence. He gives up his existence in eternity so that the beings he created may exist and know that they exist. This is the meaning of the sentence which expresses the deepest insight of the mysteries, a sentence which occurs near the end of this chapter: God is love.

This loving God is also hidden or enchanted in all the beings of nature around us. And not by looking into himself but by contemplating the phenomena of nature in the right way the human soul can come to a knowledge of God. And through this knowledge the God in the human being is awakened from the enchanted sleep. Knowledge in the sense of the mysteries was not a collection of dry, dead facts but the living experience of how the spirit in the world awakened the human spirit. It is a knowing which is at the same time a loving. When we find in Rudolf Steiner's *Knowledge of the Higher Worlds* as the first exercise the instruction to contemplate a seed, we are given an example of the way people came to knowledge in the ancient mysteries.

The divine power which rests enchanted in nature is called by Rudolf Steiner in this chapter the 'Father-God'. What is awakened in the human soul through a knowledge of the Father-God in nature is 'God, the Son'. Man finds the divine in himself by seeking the divine in the world. This was the 'immaculate conception' or the 'virgin birth' as it was understood in the mysteries. And what was born in the soul as the 'Son of God' was selfless love, a love of the same nature as that eternal love that gave existence to all things.

This is also the hidden meaning of the fable of Eros and Psyche as told by the initiate of the mysteries, Apuleius. Psyche (the soul) is married to the god of love, Eros, but he comes only at night and she is not allowed to see him. This means that the divine love element is hidden in the depths of the unconscious. When Psyche, against the command of Eros, attempts to catch a glimpse of him, he leaves her. Here the fable conveys the meaning that mere curiosity, the spur of our ordinary knowledge, only estranges the human soul from the true love of wisdom. Psyche has to fulfil several apparently impossible tasks before she is reunited with Eros. This is a hint of the ordeals of initiation. It is only by passing through the trials demanded by the mysteries that the soul can find consciously the divine element which otherwise remains unconscious. When the lovers are reunited, Zeus bestows immortality upon Psyche. The soul who has found the hidden God has also found its own immortal part.

The fable, as Apuleius tells it, is overladen with details which serve to hide the mystery meaning; that the divine in a human being is of the nature of love. Yet there were circles where this meaning was known and understood right into Christian times. This is shown by the fact that practically the same story was told as a fairy-tale by the 'heretical' Cathars and Albigenses of the Middle Ages. And in the form of the fairy-tale of the king of the ravens it survived in Provence until the nineteenth century.

The mystery secret that God is love and that the divine

in man is also love appeared, however, as his own insight in the mind of the German philosopher Fichte; perhaps it was a memory of mystery knowledge in a previous incarnation which suddenly lit up in him. In any case, the young Rudolf Steiner was overjoyed when he found the idea in one of Fichte's works and wrote to a friend:

> On my desk I've about thirty or more books by and about Fichte. I would like to write something fundamental about this great spirit for the occasion of his centenary. I have come to appreciate him more and more. This morning a passage in one of his books has filled me with utter delight:
> 'Life is love and the whole form and force of life consists of love and springs from love. In saying this I have pronounced one of the most profound statements possible to human knowledge – a statement which can become clear to any concentrated thought. Love divides, in a manner of speaking, existence which, by itself, would be lifeless. Love divides existence into a duality and thus confronts existence with itself [the duality of the divine in the world and the divine in the human being]. But love also unites and intimately connects what has been divided. This is the true nature of the "I" which, without love, could only look upon the world coldly and without interest.'
> He who understands something like this not only with dead reason but as a living experience, has awakened to a special kind of life. And only he who can do so has a real understanding of freedom. And freedom is what I aim to make the cornerstone of all my philosophy.[1]

From the ancient mysteries to the *Philosophy of Freedom* there runs a thread which has never been broken: the knowledge that God is Love.

3

Mystery Knowledge and Early Philosophy

As the first chapter of the book explained the relationship between the mysteries and the popular religions, so the next chapter shows the connection between the mysteries and the first philosophers. It was the Greek civilisation which produced the first men who tried to understand the world by means of ideas and concepts. Earlier ages had no need and felt no urge to go beyond the mythologies passed on from one generation to the next. The dawn of human thought as a means of knowing and understanding came in ancient Greece.

But the first, the pre-Socratic philosophers, used thoughts which were still imaginative pictures rather than abstract concepts. And, what is even more significant, many of these men were, in a lower or higher degree, initiates of some mystery temple. And while they did not reveal mystery secrets, they expressed in their philosophies certain views which were fundamental to all mysteries.

The greatest of these pioneers of philosophy was Heraclitus. What is known of his world conception consists only of fragments, a few sentences quoted by other authors and attributed to him. Yet even these broken shards can give us an inkling of the whole complex of his ideas. And the central element of this complex is the 'eternal'. The eternal in the sense of Heraclitus is not something static or monotonous or abstract (which is what the word conjures up in the modern mind) but something not only endowed with life, but giving life.

One has to use analogies and metaphors to get at least a little nearer to the eternal as understood by Heraclitus. If we were to stand on the seashore watching the waves rising and falling in endless succession, and we would then try to form in our mind an idea of *the* wave – something that lives in all and every wave from the tiniest wavelet to the mountainous seas of a storm – something which is manifest in every wave but is not and cannot be any one of them, then we have in this physically quite unreal 'wave' some approximation to the reality of the 'eternal' of Heraclitus. And then we can understand his saying 'all is in flux' because all that exists in the world of the senses is no more than a wave, rising, falling and gone, from the tiniest creature to the highest mountain and even the earth itself.

Because the eternal was a reality for Heraclitus he could describe it from different aspects. One of these other aspects can be understood if we imagine a tug-of-war between two teams of equal strength. For a time the rope which they pull in opposite directions will be taut and as stiff and still as a rod. But the stability of the rope is only the result of two opposing forces; the *opposition* is real, not the rigid stability of the rope. It is the same with all which we consider as stable in the world. The apparent stability is the result of the tension between opposing forces.

An example of this is Rudolf Steiner's explanation of health. In our body two kinds of forces are active: those which, by themselves, would produce inflammation and those which work towards hardening, sclerosis.[1] And the tug-of-war between these two – as long as they are of equal strength – is what we call health. Nothing can exist in the world without this kind of opposition.

The Chinese called the opposing principles yin and yang, Greek mythology called them Uranos and Gaia, in Solomon's temple they were represented by the two pillars, Jachin and Boaz.

But Heraclitus was not concerned with names for the polarities; he looked upon the relationship between them, the opposition, and said, 'War is the father of all things.' He did not mean the murderous wars between people, but the *creative* war, the creative opposition of eternal polarities. Goethe discovered the same truth when he saw the beauty of colour in the world arising from a 'battle' between light and darkness.

But how can the eternal – the all-encompassing oneness – be two? How can there be opposition within something which, by its own nature, is above all contradictions and oppositions? Heraclitus found a wonderful image and metaphor which answers this question: the *bow*. This ancient weapon of war is one piece of wood, yet the two ends hold the bowstring as taut as the two teams hold the rope in their tug-of-war. In the bow we see oneness and twoness, or opposition, reconciled. Heraclitus did not seek a rational, intellectual explanation, he had an image which demonstrated a certain aspect of the eternal, and this was enough.

The image of the bow which is a oneness and yet at the same time a polarity, a twofoldness, is also the key to other seemingly paradoxical statements of Heraclitus, such as that death and birth are one. The death in one incarnation and the birth in the following incarnation are like two ends of the bow. And the life in the spiritual world between death and rebirth, the life in the world of the eternal, is the bow. And they are all one. In the same way old age in one life and childhood in the next life are one, as they are connected by the great 'bow' of spiritual existence. And similarly physical non-existence (which begins at death) and physical existence (which begins and birth) are one.

At the time of Heraclitus there existed not only the bow as a weapon of war, but also another kind of bow with a quite different purpose: the lyre. The strings on a lyre are, in principle, not different from the single string of a bow. And the musical instrument of the lyre with its many strings provides Heraclitus with another image for the nature of the eternal.

Each string of a lyre produces a different tone and because of this difference there is the possibility of disharmony or harmony between them. Here in the sense-world, the manifoldness, the variety and the differences, can and do produce discords, but in the world of the eternal all differences are reconciled in one great harmony.

We can take this image a step further. Whether a lyre or any other instrument produces painful discords or pleasant harmonies depends on the musician who plays it. Who is the musician whose lyre is the whole world – and the strings of that lyre are all beings that exist in the world? Heraclitus called this being the Logos, the Cosmic Word. It was later taken up by the Gospel of John: 'In the beginning was the Word.'

But this whole conception of the Logos, the Cosmic Word, goes back to the mystery centres and in particular to the mystery temple of the city in which Heraclitus lived and also, five hundred years later, John, the author of the gospel. The temple of Diana in Ephesus was a centre where individuals were brought to the experience of the eternal cosmic Word. When Rudolf Steiner returned to the theme of the ancient mysteries in 1923 he devoted a special lecture to the Logos-mysteries of Ephesus,[2] the lecture ends with a mantric verse:

> Behold the Logos in the burning fire.
> Seek the answer in Diana's house.

The verse conveys the meaning that the teaching in the temple of Ephesus leads to an understanding of the beginning of the Earth-evolution when in the warmth-substance, the fire, the divine Word, the Logos, worked and formed. And this mystery knowledge that heat, 'fire', was the first physical form of the Earth, was also expressed by Heraclitus when he spoke of fire as the first of the elements. Yet this fire was not like the kind of heat we produce by mechanical means. It was not a soulless, lifeless heat but a warmth pervaded by the human soul, as the warmth within our body is pervaded by our personal soul-forces.

The 'fire' of Heraclitus is the warmth-body of the Earth, pervaded by the soul of mankind and formed by the Logos. One could say that the Logos plays upon the warmth-forces as a musician plays upon a lyre and it is through this that the warmth which is originally homogenous becomes differentiated.

And this 'playing' brings us to another profound metaphor of Heraclitus. We call the activity of making music on an instrument 'playing' the instrument. One can only admire the wisdom of the genius of language which uses the same word for the playing of an instrument as for the play of children. For the children as for the musician or for the actor who 'plays' a part in a 'play', the playing is a profoundly serious matter. And anyone who has seen how inventive children can be in their play, or artists in their playing on the stage or in a concert, knows that playing is really a creative activity. To play means to create.

This is the thought behind the image used by Heraclitus when he said, 'Eternity is a child at play ... the kingdom belongs to the child.' We have seen before that in the philosophy of Heraclitus old age and childhood are one, are only the two ends of the same bow. And, since our customary image of God is that of an old man, we have to add to it the other side: God as a child who plays. This is the profound appeal of the Christmas festival, which presents us with divinity in its other form: the little child.

We can see now what Heraclitus achieves by using ever new analogies for the eternal; it ceases to be an abstraction and becomes a living concept and, through this, a reality. Heraclitus does not 'prove' that there is something eternal, but if we follow his metaphors, not merely intellectually but with our hearts, we can feel at least something of the nature of the eternal or, as we call it, God.

Heraclitus not only speaks of the eternal in the world but also of the eternal in the human being. He contracts what he wants to convey into a sentence which, in the original, consists only of three words: *Ethos anthropos daimon. Ethos* is usually translated as the inner moral law. *Daimon* meant for the Greeks not a demon but a supernatural power. One could therefore translate the sentence as, 'A human being's ethical principles are like a supernatural (or spiritual) power.' However, Rudolf Steiner translates 'ethos' as 'destiny' and interprets the sentence as meaning that the eternal of the human being is present in his destiny. Thus the words of Heraclitus become an assertion of karma and reincarnation. Not many scholars would agree with this interpretation, but Rudolf Steiner's understanding of Heraclitus does not depend on scholarly research. He writes that one can read in the features of this philosopher a profound seriousness which shows that he possessed a knowledge at which words can only hint but cannot express. Someone who could see the features of Heraclitus would also know what he meant. The sayings of the Ephesian philosopher are cryptic, obscure, paradox from the start. We are immediately confronted with the need to look for the hidden meaning.

It is quite different with what is known about the teaching of the followers of Pythagoras. Even a twelve-year-old of normal intelligence can understand the theorem which bears his name. Nor is there anything mysterious about the fact that strings of different length have a different pitch. Here the secret or the mystery is not hidden by obscurity but by obviousness. That three plus four makes seven is obvious to anyone who can count. But the Pythagoreans saw in this simple bit of arithmetic and in its geometrical representation, a triangle over a square, the whole mystery of the human being's sevenfold nature. They felt awe and wonder at finding the proportions of the Golden Section in nature, in the human body and in the five-pointed star, the pentagram. The secret of the School of Pythagoras was that behind the quantitative aspect of numbers and measures there is a qualitative aspect. This is the eternal that is hidden behind the obviousness of mathematics. Heraclitus and Pythagoras showed two ways of expressing and at the same time hiding mystery knowledge; Heraclitus by obscurity, Pythagoras by the obvious.

4

The Awakening of Thinking in Greece

With philosophers like Heraclitus or Pythagoras something quite new makes its appearance: the use of thought to understand the world. Before the dawn of philosophy people either were satisfied with the imaginations of mythology or, for those who wanted to go deeper, there was the path of initiation in the mysteries. And the people who sought admittance to the mysteries would not have relied on their own thinking to arrive at any world conception.

What had happened to make philosophical thinking possible was the waning of the ancient imaginative faculty, the drying up of the sources which had given humanity the various mythologies. But this death of the instinctive imagination was at the same time an awakening: the awakening to thought. The Greek philosophers are the heralds of this awakening. They are pioneers of a new light in the human soul and this gives their ideas and concepts a force and vitality not to be found among philosophers today.

Yet these early practitioners of thinking were initiates of mystery temples. The conviction with which they speak does not rest upon the irrefutable logic of their conclusions but upon real spiritual experiences in the mysteries. This mystery-knowledge is also the strength of Plato's philosophy. In this lies also the difference between him and his pupil, Aristotle, the strict logician, who was not an initiate of any mystery school.

This is also the reason why Aristotle is not mentioned in *Christianity as Mystical Fact*. It is significant in this context that Plato affirmed the idea of reincarnation while Aristotle explicitly rejected it.

From his mystery experience Plato drew the conviction that there exists an immortal, eternal being in man. He tries to bring this conviction to others, not by logical argument but by speaking of the death of his venerated teacher, Socrates. The calmness and serenity with which this innocent victim of Athenian injustice accepted his fate constitutes the proof. But there is one sentence spoken by Socrates in his last hours which shows more clearly than anything else what philosophy meant at that time. He said that 'those who occupy themselves with philosophy in the right way are really – even though others will not realise it – striving after nothing else than to die – to be dead'. It is a sentence which, at least for the modern mind, is as obscure as any saying of Heraclitus. For us, speculation about matters more abstract than the problems of ordinary life is just speculation and no one engaged in it would feel it as the expression of – to use a modern term – a death wish. What does Socrates mean?

At that time ideas or concepts were not experienced as constructions of the human mind. When Socrates, in answer to people who praised his wisdom, said, 'I know only that I know nothing,' it was not because of his modesty, but because he experienced the ideas which earned him this praise as something outside himself, a light that shone into him from a higher world, the world which the human being enters after death, the world of ideas. And the world of ideas is the world of harmony, of wholeness and completeness. It is the world where the human soul is truly 'at home', the world from which we come and to which we return. And philosophic thinking in the sense in which Socrates means the word, is not idle speculation, a playing with words, but a preparation for that world.

But what are these 'ideas' which Plato regards as the living proof of the human being's own eternal, immortal being?

It is here in this chapter that Rudolf Steiner discusses the forming of ideas in a more detailed manner than anywhere else in his work. The key word in this context is 'similarity'. We see in childhood an animal in the zoo and are told that it is a lion. We later see another animal which looks so much like the first one that we also call it a lion. We have formed the *concept* 'lion', which does not mean either of the two particular lions but their similarity. One could also call it the 'design' which is the same for these two – and for all lions. We also learn that this design has to be flexible enough to include lionesses and lion cubs.

What is not considered in ordinary life, yet is all-important, is this: that the similarities, the common design, *as such,* are not physical realities – just as the likeness between two brothers is, in itself, not a physical reality. 'Likeness', 'similarity', the 'common design' express a relationship between physical realities, as does their opposite, 'unlikeness', 'difference'. And the idea 'lion' thus refers to a relationship between all lions, not to any physical reality.

In modern science the issue of this common design of all members of the same species has been blurred by misunderstanding the role of heredity. Heredity – the whole complicated system of genetics – transmits the common design; it does not create it, any more than the paper on which a letter is written creates the message contained in the letter. The common design of all lions has its origin in a supersensible being, the group-soul of the lions. And the organ by means of which we become aware of the similarity is not the physical eye but our thinking. The eye, like all the senses, reports only what is there – not whether it is related to something else or not. It is our *thinking* which 'perceives' the similarity between all lions. In other words, it is our thinking which perceives the group-soul.

At the time of Socrates and Plato the experience, 'I perceive something supersensible when I think,' was still strong enough to leave the philosophers in no doubt that what they perceived – the ideas – were realities. And when their thinking did not merely link ideas with sense-perceptions (like the idea 'lion') but linked ideas with ideas (like the idea 'human' and the idea 'morality') they felt themselves already in the supersensible realm, the realm of the eternal.

This is the experience which made Socrates say that the philosopher is already seeking death while living; he means death as the liberation from the sense-world. It is also this experience which makes the philosophic thinking of Socrates and Plato so utterly different from our own.

Yet what Plato experienced in his 'ideas' was already a mere shadow compared with the reality which humanity had known in previous epochs of evolution. There was a time when the instinctive clairvoyance reached up to the astral world. In that world the animal group-souls are as real as the human soul is real on the physical plane. What was encountered then was not the idea 'lion' but a real being, the group-soul of all lions. A remnant of this stage still existed until recently. When the Bushmen of the Kalahari Desert went antelope hunting they first held a ceremony in which they apologised to the antelope spirit for the killing of one of its earthly representatives. In ancient Atlantis clairvoyance had reached as far as lower devachan where the group-spirits of the plant forms on earth have their life and being. And when mankind lived in Lemuria the ancient clairvoyance enabled man to meet the group-souls of the mineral world in the higher devachan.

Plato's 'ideas' were therefore no more than a memory of realities which mankind had known in earlier times, but Plato knew from the teaching he had received in the mysteries that behind the sense perceptions there were not just ideas but real beings. He knew that in the minerals, plants and animals there are real spiritual beings in a state of 'enchantment'. And he expressed this knowledge in the image which is mentioned in the chapter on Plato in *Christianity as Mystical Fact*, the image of the 'world cross'. The four arms of the cross are the four kingdoms, mineral, plant, animal, man. In each of them spiritual beings are tied to matter. In this way the world-spirit is nailed to the world-cross of material existence.[1]

But mankind's relation to the world cross is different from that of other beings. As long as human beings are only aware of their physical existence, their own true spiritual nature is as hidden from them as the spiritual beings in the kingdoms of nature. But on the path of knowledge, which human souls could find in the mystery schools, they came to a realisation of the spirit in themselves and in nature. It was a path of redemption from the cross of matter.

The mysteries taught a path of *knowledge* – but the word meant something quite different from what we call knowledge. We think of it as information which is either useful or interesting for *us,* for ourselves. It would not even occur to us that it means something to the *world.* Yet this is just how the mysteries and Plato looked upon knowledge. For them the spirit hidden in matter, 'nailed to the cross', becomes manifest in human thinking and thus redeemed and awakened to new life. In the sense in which they understood it, 'knowledge' was part of a world process, a necessary part, a renewal and rebirth of the world-spirit.

This is the meaning of the words of the Neoplatonic philosopher Philo of Alexandria (a contemporary of Christ) quoted by Rudolf Steiner. The world-wisdom, the Logos, is born in the human being as the son of the Father-wisdom enchanted in the world of the senses. Philo describes his experience of philosophic thinking in words not far from religious ecstasy:

> It was as though divine power took hold of me and
> inspired me, so that I did not know where I was,
> who was with me, who I was, or what I was saying or
> writing.[2]

And Rudolf Steiner's comment on these words is that on this path of knowledge one is conscious that when the Logos becomes alive in the soul one is at one with the divine. If anyone knew and understood this experience it was the author of *The Philosophy of Freedom*. But one cannot reach such intensity in one's thinking unless one is a philosopher in the literal sense of the word: a lover of wisdom. One has to love the inner life in ideas.

Plato knew that love and built a lasting monument to it in the *Banquet* or *Symposium*. Seldom has a philosopher's idea been so misunderstood and misused as the 'Platonic love' represented in this work. In Plato's sense love is the power which brings together what was separated. In its first form a man and woman, in a higher form individual and community, in its highest form the human being and God, the human soul and the Logos.

The process of separation – the partitioning of the oneness that was in the beginning – is presented in the myth of Dionysus, the son of Zeus and Semele, who was torn to pieces by the Titans (the earthly forces). This myth was the central theme of the Orphic mysteries, where the soul was led to experience the tearing apart of the oneness. It is a process that we meet on many levels. There was, for instance, a common soul of mankind, a group-soul of mankind as there is a group-soul of lions. We are each of us a torn-away part of that soul. But, unlike the animal group-souls which stay in higher worlds, the human group-soul was born on earth in the Nathanic Jesus child who became the vessel for the Christ. This is the mystery at the heart of the Christmas festival. But Rudolf Steiner looks at another aspect of the Dionysus theme. He points to the different branches of knowledge, the different sciences in which the divine wisdom has been broken up. But by seeking the Logos, the spiritual truth, in each branch of science, we shall find the common ground, the cosmic wisdom. The whole of Rudolf Steiner's spiritual science is an illustration of the task outlined here in a few sentences. But the driving force behind his achievement was love – love for the Logos, love for the divine wisdom in nature, in the cosmos, in man. This is the Platonic love praised above all others in the *Banquet*.

Plato stood at the threshold where human thinking, though still founded on mystery knowledge, began to go its own way. Aristotle, although Plato's pupil, put his trust in the power of human thought alone, independent of any mystery teaching. A few centuries later the mystery temples had disappeared, their knowledge was lost, and thinking began to seek truth in the world of the senses, not in the world of the spirit. Rudolf Steiner stood at another threshold where thinking opens the way to the new mysteries. There is a statement in *The Philosophy of Freedom* which, as it were, heralds the new mysteries:

> Thinking all too readily leaves us cold in recollection; it is as if the life of the soul had dried out. Yet this is really nothing but the strongly marked shadow of its real nature – warm, luminous, and penetrating deeply into the phenomena of the world. This penetration is brought about by a power flowing through the activity of thinking itself – the power of love in its spiritual form.[3]

Plato would have understood it. The ancient mysteries would have understood it. We children of the present age must learn to understand it.

5

The Interpretation of Ancient Myths

We have seen that for Plato the mysteries knowledge was not something which concerned only the individual who acquired it, or humanity which may benefit from it, but was a cosmic process, a process involving the divine beings and their creation, the cosmos. And a philosopher like Plato looked upon the myths of gods and heroes as nothing less than an older form of knowledge, a form which was itself the work of divine beings. Thus the interpretation of the ancient myths as it was taught in the mystery schools, or as Plato undertakes in some of his dialogues, is the act of making conscious what divine wisdom has given the human soul unconsciously in the images of mythology. Such interpretation was not a debunking (which is the attitude of the modern mind when it deals with myth and legend) but was undertaken in a spirit of reverence for the work of the gods.

The process which led from the ancient reverence for 'knowledge' to the irreverence of the present was described by Rudolf Steiner in a lecture given in Vienna. This description is itself a myth in the sense of Plato and the mysteries:

> Today, in our present cycle of evolution, we say: 'I
> think.' Those who knew of these things in earlier times
> would say: 'The gods think in us' when visions came
> from the world of spirit ... 'Human beings ... are the

stage for the divine thoughts.' People knew themselves to be filled with these thoughts and therefore said: 'The gods think in me.'

Human evolution demanded, however, that this became increasingly less possible. We might say that increasing darkness met the visions and thoughts of the gods in the human being ... A time was approaching when thoughts would no longer come from human beings to meet the gods. The divine entity who may be said to have been thinking through the human being felt that its consciousness, which consisted in its thoughts, was growing dull and fading away. A longing then arose in this divine entity to awaken to life a new form of consciousness. Human beings merely come to a different form of consciousness. The gods create something essential to themselves when they create a new consciousness. Christ was the essential principle to arise for the divine entity of which we are speaking when it felt its consciousness fading. Christ is the child of the divine entity and Christ restores consciousness of divine nature in human life and activity.[1]

This 'myth' tells us how it came about that man could no longer feel reverence for the thoughts that came to him. It can also make us aware that we do not understand the Christ-impulse unless we treat certain thoughts, the thoughts we find in anthroposophy, with reverence – for they are the thoughts of a divine being. And we shall then also feel reverence for the ancient mythologies.

The myths referred to in this chapter of *Christianity as Mystical Fact* are all variations of a single theme: initiation. They tell stories about certain heroes and their battles with all kinds of monsters. These monsters represent the forces in the human soul which have to be overcome on the path of initiation and the battles refer to the inner struggle which everyone who enters upon this path has to fight. Within ourselves live both the hero and the monsters.

Most people are only vaguely aware of these two sides of human nature. In the mystery schools the pupils were made acutely conscious of the hero and the beast in their own souls, and 'initiation', the process in which the spirit of the human being is united with the spirit of the world, came to those who had, at least to some extent, gained control over the crude instincts and desires. They also learned that there comes for every human soul the time when the hero must consciously confront the monsters. Some come to it earlier, others later, but every soul is destined to take up the struggle and eventually to become an 'initiate'.

Initiation was in the past something that was only possible for a relatively small number: it will in the future become the obligation of every human soul. This is the reason why anthroposophy has come into the world: to prepare souls for this future. This is also the reason why so much of Rudolf Steiner's work deals with initiation. It is not something which concerns a small minority but something that concerns and will concern everybody; initiation is the karma which awaits everyone. And the stories which tell us of heroes slaying giants, dragons, monstrous hybrids, are therefore images of our own future karma. The myth speaks of the past but foretells the future.

The myth of Theseus – the first one to which Rudolf Steiner refers in this chapter on mysteries and myth – can be understood in this sense. Minos, the king of Crete, had subjugated the city of Athens. Every year the Athenians had to send seven young men and seven maidens to Crete as a tribute demanded by Minos. There they were forced to enter a maze, the labyrinth, where they got lost and could not find a way out. Finally a monster with the head of a bull and the body of a man, the Minotaur, devoured them. Theseus was the hero who came to free Athens from the tyranny of King Minos. He accompanied the next group of youngsters sent to the island of Crete. The task he had set himself, to slay the Minotaur, was made easier by the help of Ariadne, the daughter of Minos, who fell in love with him. It was her advice which enabled Theseus to find his way through the labyrinth and to overcome the bull-man.

The myth can be interpreted by regarding Minos as the power which holds sway over us as long as we cling to the world of the senses. It is this power which devours all the 'young' forces, the forces of potential spiritual development. We have to awaken in us the hero, Theseus, who is helped by Ariadne; that means higher knowledge, spiritual knowledge. Armed with this knowledge the hero penetrates to the depth where the monster lurks and overcomes the desires, passions and urges which bind the soul to the world of the senses. Then the soul has gained inner freedom – as Athens was freed from the oppression of Minos.

Rudolf Steiner's interpretation as given in this chapter is along these lines. However, simply by speaking of this myth immediately after the chapter on Plato and Socrates, names which are forever linked with Athens, Rudolf Steiner put up a signpost which says, 'Look for the connection of this myth with the development of philosophic thought in Athens.' Since European civilisation would not be what it is without this contribution, without the concepts formulated first by Socrates, Plato, Aristotle in Athens, the myth of Theseus, the cult-hero of Athens speaks, in fact, of the birth of a new impulse in the history of mankind. This is another meaning of the story of Theseus, Ariadne and the Minotaur.

The great initiates whose spiritual achievements are represented in the images of myth have a still higher task than the overcoming of demons in their souls; they have to bring new impulses into the world. Before new faculties can arise in human beings generally, there have first to be individuals who develop these faculties in themselves, well in advance of the rest of mankind. An example of such a faculty is compassion. Today any normal human being is capable of being touched by the suffering of others. Yet, if the Gautama Buddha had not lived 2,500 years ago and if he had not made his being the soil in which the first seed of compassion could be planted, there would still be no sense of pity for others in human beings. The great initiates are the pioneers of mankind's real progress, spiritual progress.

The Theseus myth tells the story of such an initiate and pioneer of mankind. The myth is not concerned with the earthly personality who became the bearer of the new impulse; it is not concerned with his 'biography' but with the impulse itself and with the forces which opposed it. Whenever something new comes into the world it is opposed by the protagonists of the old order. This recurrent theme in the history of mankind is also present in this saga.

Minos and his bull-headed ogre represent the human soul-forces as they were at the time when the spring equinox was in the sign of Taurus, the Bull. This was the age of the Egyptian and Babylonian civilisations. In Greece, the Taurus impulse had its centre on the island of Crete; the archaeological remains of that period show to what an extent life on Crete was dominated by the cult of the Bull.

The characteristic feature of the Taurus-age (the epoch of the sentient soul) was that people felt themselves as part of their national or tribal group-spirit and that they were guided by group instincts. The bull, Taurus, is the symbol for the wisdom of the instinctive forces. But when the spring equinox passed into the sign of Aries the Ram, the time of the forces of the rational soul had come; the time when the single personality should assert itself and when human reason should replace the dependence on instincts and instinctive clairvoyance. Theseus is the hero of the emerging new Aries forces. In another saga about his deeds it is said that he took part in the Argonauts' quest for the Golden Fleece, which is an image of the impulse of Aries, the Ram.

In order to awaken the light of reason, of rational thinking, Theseus has to overcome the instinctive Bull forces.

He could not accomplish this task without the help of Ariadne. Who is Ariadne? She is the spirit-self or manas. Although human beings will develop manas or the spirit-self in a later epoch, this higher self has been present in the spiritual world since the beginning of earth evolution. The initiates of the mysteries could reach this higher self and be inspired by it to undertake the tasks they had to accomplish. A necessary part of preparing the future manas stage was the development of the faculty of clear, logical thinking. Ariadne, the spirit-self, tells Theseus what he had to do in order to understand the world not by instinct but by thought. The myth expresses Ariadne's advice in a profound image; she gives Theseus a ball of thread to aid him in his passage through the labyrinth. He ties one end of the thread to the entrance of the maze and rolls it as he penetrates into the interior; thus he can always find his way back.

The labyrinth is an imagination for the human brain with its many convolutions. For the ancient instinctive knowledge, the brain was not of great importance; but for the new forces of reason and thinking the physical instrument of the brain is essential. Theseus had to learn (and mankind as a whole had to learn) to use the brain – which means to think in abstract concepts instead of having the imaginations of instinctive knowledge. And what is the thread which guides Theseus safely through the labyrinth? It is logic, the logical connection of one thought with another. This is the great achievement which brain-thinking brought to mankind: the objectivity of logical thinking. And in that light of logic there shines already – and preparing the way for it – the wisdom of manas, the spirit-self. Logic is the gift of Ariadne.

But why in the myth is Ariadne a daughter of Minos, the representative of the group-soul forces in the epoch of the Bull? Because in that epoch manas was at one with the group-souls. The spirit-self, the higher self, could not yet work through individuals – it had to work with the group-souls and through the group-souls. And because manas was at that time at one with the group-souls, the king who symbolises this older stage of evolution is called 'Minos' which is the same word as 'manas'. But with the new age dawning, the spirit-self separates from the group-souls and seeks to express itself through the single personality, Theseus. This is the reality behind the myth that Ariadne helps Theseus against her own father – that means against the previous condition of the spirit-self.

Theseus embarks with the young Athenians he has saved and with Ariadne on the journey back to Athens. He intends to marry her. But a storm drives the ship to the island of Naxos and there the goddess Pallas Athene appears to Theseus and tells him that Ariadne is not for him. She is destined to be the bride of the god Dionysus and Theseus must leave her behind on the island.

To understand this part of the myth we have to remember that Theseus came to Ariadne, the spirit-self, through the mystery-tradition. The time when mystery knowledge could be taken into the outer world had not yet come. The rational, logical thinking which Theseus was to bring had to become separated from mystery knowledge. In Heraclitus, Pythagoras, Socrates and Plato, philosophic thought still retains a connection with mystery wisdom, but this is only of short duration – as was the connection between Theseus and Ariadne. With Aristotle there comes already the break with any mystery tradition – and ever since, human thought has developed its own strength, independent of the mysteries. It is only in our time, in anthroposophy, that the spiritual knowledge of the mysteries can be brought into human thought. This is the marriage of Ariadne and Dionysus, the god who represents the intellect.

But at the time when the spring equinox was in Aries, the time of the Greek civilisation, thought had to be emancipated from the mysteries – and this is what the myth of Theseus and Ariadne conveys. It was in Athens, the city of Theseus, where this emancipation of human thinking began. Our task is to bring together again what was separated in Athens: logical thought and mystery knowledge.

6

A Buddhist Fable and the Myth of Osiris

As we have seen, the myth of Theseus and the Minotaur can be understood on two different levels. Taken in its historical context, the myth describes the moment in evolution when conscious thought (Theseus) freed itself from the dominion of the instincts (the Minotaur), but the story can also be interpreted as presenting a pattern which applies to all souls who strive towards the spirit; the timeless pattern of initiation, which demands the subduing of the lower nature by the higher self. One has to realise that all true imaginations can be interpreted in several ways, yet each one of them is true. In Rudolf Steiner's work, Michael's fight with the dragon means one thing in the context of the four seasons and the archangels, it means something quite different as an image of the battle for human intelligence described in the Michael Letters (also known as *Anthroposophical Leading Thoughts*).

Michael's fight with the dragon is altogether the archetypal image for the two tendencies in every human soul: there is something in us which wants to become better and wiser than we are and there is something which wants to prevent this from happening. One becomes aware of these adversary forces as soon as one takes the very first step towards the higher self, the practice of meditation. Rudolf Steiner tells in this chapter a Buddhist fable which describes with great precision the forces which oppose one's efforts to meditate.

The fable speaks of a man whose life is endangered by five assassins, by four poisonous snakes and by a single executioner who wants to decapitate him with a sword. The 'life' in danger is the man's spiritual life, which needs meditation. And the first enemies who threaten this life, the five assassins, are the five senses. Any noise from outside can break one's concentration, and so can smells or changes of the light. It may seem at times that the whole world of the senses is one great conspiracy to prevent meditation. The task becomes even harder if one happens to be in the grip of a strong emotion – anxiety, grief, passionate love or hatred. This is, in the fable, the man bent on cutting off one's head. We do indeed 'lose our head' when such emotions gain hold of us and it needs great will-power to rise in meditation above such astral storms.

Even more insidious are the adversaries symbolised by the four poisonous snakes which, so we are told, are the four elements, fire, air, water, earth. How can the elements interfere with meditation? In the form of the four temperaments. Although one temperament is usually predominant, there are in every one of us all four present – and they make this presence felt. The choleric gets impatient with the slow rate of progress, the sanguine gets bored with the repetitive nature of this work, the phlegmatic insists that it does not matter whether one meditates or not and the melancholic is convinced of his own unworthiness – so why bother? There is a painting by the fifteenth-century artist Hieronymus Bosch which depicts four soldiers pressing the crown of thorns on the head of Christ. The four soldiers are clearly characterised as the four temperaments. But Christ's untroubled countenance proclaims the inner power which is immune to the attacks of the temperaments.

Eventually the man in the Buddhist fable escapes from murderers and snakes. He comes to a village which is deserted; all its inhabitants have left. This is an image of our memory pictures, our reminiscences, which recall a past but contain nothing of the reality of that past. The things we remember can also hinder us in keeping the mind concentrated on the subject of our meditation.

At last the man builds himself a boat from straw, twigs and leaves. These flimsy materials seem quite unlikely to provide the means to make a boat which could cross a river – no more than the flimsy substance of our thoughts seems a likely vehicle to carry the soul from the sense-world to the world of the spirit. And to begin with, our meditation, whether it be a symbol an image or a mantra, is no more than a thought, as flimsy and insubstantial as all our other thoughts. It is our will-power, patience and persistence which make mere thoughts into a reality strong enough to cross the stream which separates the sense-world from the spirit.

The battle against the demons of myth and saga begins with the trials and tribulations one encounters as soon as one makes the first steps in meditation. The Buddhist fable speaks in its own quiet way of the same struggle as the epics which celebrate the deeds of great heroes. The inner quietness of meditation is already a triumph over the demons. The German mystic Angelus Silesius expressed this thought in the words:

> When stillness reigns in you, all inner turmoil gone,
> St Michael has a battle against the dragon won.

The daily little victories in the practice of meditation are already part of the great struggle between Michael and the dragon. But the struggle in which the soul is engaged on this path is not only a battle *against* something, against obstructions of one kind or another, it is above all a striving *for* something. The aim of this striving is expressed in the Egyptian Osiris myth.

The human soul finds itself as a single separate entity in a sense-world of single, separate objects and beings. And in the soul a need as powerful as the physical needs of hunger or thirst arises – the need to overcome this fragmentation.

There would be no science if it were not for the inner need to establish connections between separate phenomena, such as the connection between the growth of plants and sunlight or between the tides and the moon. There would be no art without the inner need to create something in which all parts are interconnected to form a wholeness, be it in the colours of a painting, the tones of a piece of music or the words of a poem. And there would be no religion without the inner need to establish a connection between the separate individual soul and a higher, all-encompassing totality. Science, art and religion are in their different ways expressions of the same need. But science, art and religion can only *speak* of this oneness; they cannot provide the soul with a direct experience of it. Initiation is the way to find this experience.

The Egyptian god Osiris can be understood as representing the original oneness and wholeness of all existence. The process which led to the isolated fragments the soul encounters in the sense-world is described in the myth as the deed of Typhon who killed Osiris and tore him to pieces. What we see around us as single entities – people, animals, plants, mountains and rivers, the stars in the sky – are all 'pieces' of the dismembered Osiris. Even the soul itself is such a fragment of Osiris. This is the reason why the Egyptian mysteries called human bodies the 'coffins of Osiris'. But Isis, the sister and widow of Osiris, gathered the fragments and joined them together. Isis represents esoteric knowledge, mystery knowledge. It is a knowledge which rises above the sense-world. As long as observation and thinking remain bound to the sense-world, the fragmentation cannot be overcome. The fact that our materialistic science is breaking up into ever more specialised divisions and subdivisions demonstrates clearly that moving in this direction leads only deeper into the realm of Typhon or, as Rudolf Steiner called him, Ahriman.

It is spiritual science, the mystery knowledge of our time, which can establish true interrelationships between the phenomena as did the mystery knowledge of ancient times.

This is the goddess Isis, or Isis-Sophia as Rudolf Steiner called her. And in the soul that cultivates the Isis-Sophia knowledge, the original oneness is reborn in a new form, represented in the myth by Horus, the son of Isis and Osiris. The Isis-Sophia knowledge is not – as our ordinary knowledge is – a sum of useful or interesting or edifying information which could be gathered and stored in a computer. When the Isis-Sophia knowledge lives in the soul, as real understanding, it engenders new forces, spiritual forces. This is Horus, the god of the rising sun, who overcomes Typhon-Ahriman. The Isis-Osiris-Horus myth is as true today as it was in ancient Egypt. When Rudolf Steiner states in his first 'Leading Thought', 'Anthroposophy is a path of knowledge, to guide the spiritual in the human being to the spiritual in the universe,'[1] he expresses in a contemporary form what the Osiris myth wants to convey: the seeking of the oneness from which we have been separated.

This was also the aim of the Greek philosopher Empedocles. For him the original oneness had, first of all, been divided into the four elements. In his view all things and beings in the world are mixtures of fire, water, air and earth. The elements come together to form this or that entity and then they separate and the entity is no more. The coming together is due to the force of love between the elements; the separation is due to hatred. This view contains a profound insight. The power which separates, divides, splits up – the power which the Egyptians called Typhon – is hatred. And hatred has, as Rudolf Steiner explained, a necessary function in the universe. Without hatred there could be no difference, no variety, no distinction between beings in the world. But the force which can create out of variety a harmony – that means a new oneness – is love. The Isis of the Egyptian myth is a higher form of love; it is this love which can give birth to Horus.

Empedocles was also aware of another mystery truth: that our ordinary self has to die in order that the new self, Horus, can arise. But he took this death of the lower self in a literal and physical sense and threw himself into the crater of the volcano Etna.

Imaginations are true in the same sense as fairy-tales are true, but one would turn this truth into a lie if one were to expect some real frog to be an enchanted prince.

It should also not be assumed that myths like the tale of Isis and Osiris are merely apt parables thought up by human ingenuity – it is the spiritual world which speaks in such images. This is the reason why there is more in each myth than any particular interpretation in the form of thought. There is a spiritual life in the ancient myths which makes them meaningful beyond the time and place where they were first told. One could say that the gods are poets, and myth is their form of poetry.

7

The Myth of Heracles

The next myth to which Rudolf Steiner refers has as its hero Heracles (in Latin, Hercules), whose name became a symbol for superhuman strength. The Old Testament too tells a story of someone whose physical strength seems miraculous, Samson. Both tales hint at a spiritual truth – at the secret of the human will.

We can observe a man lifting a heavy object and we can see the same task performed by some mechanical contrivance such as a crane. For materialistic science the force is the same whether it is used by the man or by the machine. But in reality the force used by the man is different in kind from the energy which activates the mechanism. In the lectures on curative education Rudolf Steiner makes the surprising statement that every act of will, even something as normal as walking, is magic.[1] What is meant by 'magic' is the use of spiritual forces to produce physical effects. And the forces which move my legs when I walk *are* spiritual forces. They are the forces of the I. In any action performed by my physical body the I is present in the form of will. But the I is a spiritual entity and human will is a spiritual force.

In every act of will, spiritual forces are transformed into physical energy. This is demonstrated by a fact which is well known but little understood. A maniac in a raving fit is so strong that it takes several men to hold him. As Rudolf Steiner explained, it is the ego of the madman which bursts out with such terrible strength. Normally these forces remain unconscious. In fact the whole complex of human will is unconscious. In the case of the maniac, normal consciousness is obliterated and the unconscious powers rise to the surface and become manifest. There are other rather dubious ways of tapping this source of energy. Hypnotised persons can perform feats of strength they would not be capable of in waking consciousness. But this method of unleashing hidden energies was permissible in the past and was the secret of the builders of the Great Pyramid. Their workforce moved the enormous blocks of stone under a kind of mass hypnosis.[2]

The tremendous strength which is – one could say – 'stored' in the I is, of course, not intended to be used physically over and above the needs of normal life. It is intended to serve our spiritual development. This was the use made of these forces in the ancient mystery centres. The path of initiation demanded more will, more inner strength than is required of us in ordinary life. And as Theseus can be regarded as an initiate of thought, so Heracles is the initiate of will. What the myth presents as deeds of physical strength is meant to convey the spiritual powers required in the initiation of will.

Yet there is, as has been pointed out before, a connection between the spiritual strength of Heracles and the physical strength of a raving maniac. This connection is indicated in the myth. Heracles marries a king's daughter and has several children with her. But the goddess Hera, who is his arch enemy, strikes him with madness and he kills his own children. When he has regained his sanity he imposes upon himself the famous 'twelve labours' to atone for his crime. Unless it is devoted to spiritual development, the strength possessed by the I can become, and must become, destructive – as it is in madness. Much of the destructive and self-destructive tendencies of the present age are the result of unused forces of the I.

This 'killing of the children' is, however, to be taken as an image of the task of Heracles. The children represent the forces of the future as they exist in the I. When someone draws on these forces before their time, when they are used at an earlier stage, they are lost for the soul's future development.

This is the 'killing of the children' – and it was done by Heracles as a *sacrifice*. He had to make this sacrifice in order to bring into Greek civilisation a will-impulse which it needed.

Heracles was a cult hero of the Greek Olympic Games. It is *his* impulse which lived in Greek gymnastics, in the Greek enjoyment of athletic pursuits. But this was something utterly different from anything which is now practised as sport. The Greek gymnasts experienced the harmony of the physical body, and the physical harmony was at the same time spiritual. When they used their physical strength they felt at the same time the spiritual origin of this strength; for them the body was indeed a 'temple of the gods'. It was this experience which also found expression in Greek art. Never, before or after the flowering of Greek sculpture, has the beauty of the human body found a more perfect expression.

The experience of the human body as 'temple of the gods' – this was the aim of the Heracles impulse. And this aim is closely connected with the Mystery of Golgotha. The time when the Sun Spirit, Christ, incarnated in the human body was the time when the body was felt as a temple of the divine. The Heracles impulse was a preparation for the coming of the Sun Spirit. And the Heracles myth points to this connection with the Sun Spirit by speaking of the twelve labours the hero had to accomplish. They correspond to the twelve signs of the zodiac through which the sun passes in the course of the year. Heracles is a 'sun hero' preparing the coming of the Sun Spirit.

One of the tasks of Heracles is the cleaning of the stables of King Augeas. Hundreds of head of cattle live in these stables. The dung of the animals has never been taken away. Heracles digs a channel from a nearby river through the stables, then dams the river so that it flows through the stables and carries the dung away. This task is an image for the purification of the astral body. And the cattle are an indication that this labour corresponds to the constellation Taurus, the Bull.

Another task is the hunting of the golden hind of the goddess Artemis. Heracles has to catch the hind without hurting it and so cannot use bow and arrow. He follows the animal steadfastly day and night without rest, until eventually it is exhausted and can be taken. Then Heracles brings the hind unharmed to the temple of the goddess. The hunting of the golden hind is the pursuit of truth; it allows for no shortcuts (bow and arrow) and must be alive, for a dead truth is no truth at all. But when it is found, one does not own it; truth belongs to the gods. This 'hunt' corresponds to the hunting sign Sagittarius, the Archer.

But the task which Rudolf Steiner mentions first among the labours of Heracles (and it is significant that he does) is the one concerned with Cerberus, the three-headed dog which guards the underworld. The underworld in the Greek sense means, first of all, the world into which souls enter after death; but it means also the world of the unconscious in us. After death, all this unconscious life, all that we have experienced in our sleep, becomes conscious. So the realm of the unconscious and the world of the dead are the same. Why is the world of the unconscious closed to us? Because there is a being who prevents us from becoming aware of sides of our nature we could not bear to see. This being is the Guardian of the Threshold. And the three-headed hound at the gates of the underworld is a symbol for both: for the forbidding powers of the Guardian of the Threshold and for the kind of image of ourselves we would have to face. The three heads of the monster are thinking, feeling and willing, in so far as they are earth-bound, clinging to the sense-world and inimical to the spirit. Heracles has to bring this unconscious experience to his waking consciousness. This is what is meant by his task to bring Cerberus up from the underworld. It is the meeting with the Guardian of the Threshold. This task corresponds to the sign Capricorn, the Goat, the sign of the darkest time of the year.

We can understand that in the course of initiation the soul has to learn to look back upon past stages of evolution. Heracles has reached the stage at which he is given the task of bringing some golden apples from the garden of the Hesperides.

This garden is the same as the one called Paradise in the Old Testament – and the golden apples mean a consciousness of immortality. There was once a time when mankind had a cosmic consciousness, not an earthly one, and in that cosmic existence there is change, but no death; this was the Paradise which man lost through the Luciferic temptation. But the expulsion from Paradise was not really a sudden event. It was a gradual process, and human souls retained for quite some time an awareness of their cosmic, spiritual nature; they felt themselves connected with the cosmos and not with earth.

When was the last time that human souls knew themselves as immortal cosmic beings? It was during the Atlantean epoch of earth evolution. In Atlantis human beings still felt that their earthly body carried a cosmic entity, their soul. Greek mythology retained a memory of this stage in the figure of the giant Atlas, who carries the cosmos on his shoulders. It is an image of Atlantean man whose physical body carried a cosmic consciousness – and the name 'Atlas' is a direct and unmistakable reference to Atlantis. So when Heracles has to find the golden apples of the Hesperides, which represent the cosmic consciousness of immortality, he has to regain a consciousness as it had been in Atlantis. This is what is meant when the myth tells us that Heracles went to the giant Atlas and that Atlas brought him the golden apples. Because this task involves going back in time, it corresponds to the sign Cancer, the Crab, a creature which proceeds backwards as the sun begins to move back from its highest noon position when it enters this sign.

It is not necessary to go through all the twelve labours of Heracles and to provide a detailed interpretation of these symbolic deeds. The examples given are sufficient to show that these heroic feats describe experiences on the path of initiation. As mentioned before, it is a particular initiation – the initiation of the will. This is indicated in the myth by attributing great physical strength to the hero. But there is a very significant indication right at the beginning of the myth, when the hero is still in his cradle. The goddess Hera is already then bent on destroying the child and sends two snakes to kill him in his sleep, but the baby wakens in time, takes the two snakes in his hands and strangles them. The I is the 'baby' among the four members of the human organisation, the youngest and least developed, yet it is the I – and not the other members – which has the power to overcome the Luciferic and Ahrimanic forces represented by the two snakes. Lucifer and Ahriman, beings whose wisdom and powers are far above any human capacity, are powerless before the I. Heracles is the hero who prepares the way for the coming of the I-forces at the Mystery of Golgotha.

8

The Golden Fleece

Initiation is the path which leads the human spirit to the world spirit. But it is also the road on which impulses from the spiritual world flow into the evolution of mankind. We understand the heroes of the various myths only if we see in them the bearers of specific impulses. Thus Theseus, who finds his way through the labyrinth, is the hero of thought, and the Theseus-impulse found its special expression in Athens. Heracles, who excels in feats of strength, is the hero of the will-forces, which were specially cultivated in Sparta. There were still other impulses working in Greece, such as the Orphic mysteries and the mysteries of Eleusis. The mystery centres from which the various impulses flowed were each bound up with a certain locality. This is the reason why individuals with a deep interest in spiritual knowledge had to travel far and wide. What could be found in the temple of Ephesus was different from anything to be learned at Eleusis.

However, if the Greek civilisation was to fulfil its particular mission (it became, as we know, the cradle of European civilisation) the various localised impulses had to become servants of a higher common purpose – of a destiny greater than even that of Greece itself. Such a spiritual event took place, the subordination of the separate mystery impulses to one of a higher order. The myth describing this spiritual event in imaginations is the voyage of the Argonauts (among them Theseus and Heracles) and the aim of their voyage, the gaining of the Golden Fleece, is the symbol of the higher impulse.

The Golden Fleece represents cosmic forces coming from the constellation Aries, the Ram. When the spring equinox passed from the sign Taurus to the sign Aries, a new epoch, the fourth post-Atlantean epoch, began: the age in which the rational soul was to be developed in humanity. Greek civilisation – and that means the spiritual impulses of the Greek mystery centres – had to become subordinated to an impulse which encompassed all mankind, the Aries impulse. That a small community like Greece exerted such an enormous influence on European civilisation for so many centuries is due to this mighty cosmic current which imbued Greek art and philosophy and gave them a meaning beyond the limitations of their time and location.

Jason, the leader of the Golden Fleece venture, has to accomplish two tasks: tame two fire-breathing bulls so that he can use them to plough a field, and sow in this field dragon's teeth from which fierce armed men grow who promptly fight and kill each other. These are images for the rational soul element in mankind. The rational soul stands in the middle, between the sentient soul, which had been developed earlier, and the consciousness soul, which was to come later. The fire-breathing bulls (like the bull-headed Minotaur in the Theseus myth) represent the instinctive forces of the sentient soul, which have to come under the human being's conscious control. The armed men bent on fighting each other represent certain self-destructive tendencies in the consciousness soul with which we of the present age are all too familiar. The rational soul had to find a balance between these forces of past and future.

Rudolf Steiner called the soul-element which began in ancient Greece *Verstandes- und Gemütsseele,* which means a combination of reason with inner warmth. The soul-warmth is a refinement, or taming, of the cruder forces of the previous sentient soul development. The clarity of reason in Greek philosophy is an anticipation (and a softening) of the harsh intellectual forces that the later consciousness soul development would bring.

Jason, having achieved this balance between past and future stages of evolution, was now ready to obtain the Golden Fleece, which means to become the bearer of the Aries impulse. What is the nature of the forces connected with the sign Aries? In the cycle of the year, Aries is the sign of spring, the sign which proclaims a new beginning. In traditional astrology, people who have Aries strongly in their horoscope are called pioneers, enthusiasts for what is new.

The civilisation which emerged in Greece brought something new simply by the fact that it was the first European civilisation. All previous ones – in India, Persia, Babylon, Egypt – had not grown on the continent of Europe. And Greek civilisation was new also in its message; it valued and praised the human being's earthly existence. This is the impulse which the myth presents in the symbol of the Golden Fleece – the impulse which began when the spring equinox entered the sign of Aries, the Ram.

The time of the sign of Aries at the spring equinox is above everything else, however, the time when the Sun Spirit, Christ, entered earthly existence – he who said, 'Behold, I make all things anew.' And when John the Baptist calls him the Lamb of God, he pays tribute to the same forces which the myth calls the Golden Fleece, the forces of the Ram, the sign of the new beginning. The myth of Jason and the Golden Fleece expresses a particular phase in the evolution of mankind, the sphere of the development of the rational soul. It is the fourth or middle epoch among the seven phases or epochs of the post-Atlantean stage of evolution. We live in the fifth epoch and there are two more to follow.

The nature and mission of the *whole* post-Atlantean development, from ancient India to the end of the seventh epoch, is expressed in the myth of Prometheus. One could say that the Prometheus myth is on a higher level and encompasses a wider part of evolution than the myth of the Golden Fleece. The Prometheus-impulse expresses the destiny of mankind over the whole time from the end of Atlantis to the future War of All Against All.

Prometheus and his brother Epimethius represent – as their names indicate – two kinds of thinking: thinking ahead, forward thinking (Prometheus) and thinking which looks backwards (Epimethius). But he who thinks forward has to imagine or invent something which is not yet here, something which does not yet exist. Thus Prometheus is the inventor. Mankind's first invention, how to make fire and how to use fire, is the gift of Prometheus.

In ancient Atlantis human beings had no inventive abilities. They could make things of a quite complicated kind, but they did this instinctively, as birds build nests or spiders spin their webs. It was only after the Atlantean period of evolution that people developed the ingenuity which began with knowing how to use fire and led eventually to space rockets and computers. However, all these inventions were made to serve selfish desires and for purely material benefits; they contributed nothing to mankind's moral or spiritual progress. This is the reason why the spiritual world (represented in the myth by Zeus) limited man's inventive powers so that he could only use them to work with dead mineral substances. If the human race had been allowed to invent living organisms, the egotistic desires would have created monsters of all kinds. But there will come a time in a distant future when human souls will be sufficiently purified to work in the organic world as they do now in inorganic matter. This binding of invention to the lifeless mineral world is expressed in the myth by having Prometheus, at the command of Zeus, chained to a rock. A vulture comes every day to gnaw at his liver, it is a symbol of the selfishness which consumes our forces.

Another measure taken by Zeus against mankind and human inventions was that he ordered Hephaistos (Vulcan) to make from metal an artificial human being, a beautiful woman called Pandora, the 'all-giving'. She brought a box of gifts to Epimethius, who – against the advice of Prometheus – opened the lid, and out flew, like clouds of insects, countless forms of illness, of pains and debilities which have tormented mankind ever since. Only the white dove of hope remained in the box.

Vulcan is the seventh and last stage of evolution. In that stage humanity will be able to work, with spiritual forces, directly into physical matter and thus to create their own physical body. The mechanical inventions of the present age anticipate in some measure forces which belong to this distant future. By using these forces mankind comes into contact with Ahriman, whose aim it is to bring future stages prematurely into the present. The spiritual world has only one way of protecting humanity against coming too much under Ahriman's influence: physical illness. What appears in the myth as a punishment is, in reality, a protective measure of the gods against Ahriman. But the fact remains that with any mechanical inventions, from the flint knife to the jet plane, we enter a sphere where Ahriman holds power and we need the compensating forces of physical illness to pay for our trespassing on his ground. Pandora with her box of tricks seems a very apt image for technology and what it does to us.

Yet the Prometheus-impulse, the development of a thinking which conceives something that does not yet exist, the inventive genius of mankind, had to come. It is the mission of the whole post-Atlantean epoch, from Ancient India to the War of All Against All, to evolve this capacity. But the mechanical devices it has produced do not express its full potential – its real aim, its true fulfilment, is something different altogether. The myth expresses this by telling us that Heracles comes to the rock where Prometheus lies chained. The hero shoots the vulture with one of his arrows, frees Prometheus from his chains and reconciles him with Zeus. A centaur, half man, half animal, takes the place of Prometheus on the rock. What this allegory of Prometheus Unbound means is a transformation of the 'forward thinking', of the thinking which conceives something which is not yet here. When this thinking is freed from selfishness (the shooting of the vulture) it conceives moral impulses – it becomes what Rudolf Steiner in the *Philosophy of Freedom* calls moral fantasy, moral intuition and moral technique *(moralische Phantasie,* sometimes translated as 'moral imagination'). Human beings – if they are to be truly 'free' – invent the moral impulses; they invent the moral tasks they will perform.

Henri Dunant witnessed the aftermath of a battle and conceived something that did not exist – the organisation which later became known as the Red Cross. This is an example of a man's forward thinking directed towards moral inventions instead of mechanical ones. The fact that Rudolf Steiner in this context uses the words 'moral technique' shows that this kind of thinking is akin to technical concepts. It is 'Prometheus Unbound'. Not everyone will have intuitions on a grand scale like Dunant, but everyone can have intuitions which can be realised, can become facts, if one gets rid of the vulture of selfishness and has the strength of will (Heracles) to follow one's intuition. In everyone there is a Prometheus waiting to be freed. The centaur who is chained to the rock is our 'lower self', our shortcomings and failings which are still a part of us, besides the Prometheus in the soul.

In ancient times only the high initiates of the mysteries could reach the source of all moral intuitions, the Sun Spirit. In the Mystery of Golgotha this spirit has united itself with the earth and the light of moral fantasy can shine into every soul.

9

Odysseus

The Prometheus myth speaks, in the language of imaginations, of mankind's task in the long era of the seven post-Atlantean epochs – to develop individual freedom. The binding and unbinding of Prometheus expresses the descent into matter and the ascent to the spirit, which are necessary to achieve this end. Each one of the seven post-Atlantean epochs is a specific stage in this process. The myth of Jason and the Golden Fleece represents one of these stages, the fourth, the epoch of the rational soul. There is also a myth which can be regarded as expressing the following epoch, the age of the consciousness soul, our own time. It is the myth of Odysseus.

As the sentient soul was developed under the sign of Taurus, the Bull, the rational soul under the sign of Aries, the Ram, so the consciousness soul is connected with the spring equinox in the sign of Pisces, the Fish. The Odysseus saga hints at this connection by making the hero a seafarer and all his adventures happen on a sea-journey. It is not an accident that at the dawn of the consciousness soul in the fifteenth century, the mythological travels of Odysseus were echoed in the great voyages of discovery.

Odysseus is the hero who brought the Trojan War to a victorious conclusion for the Greeks by the ruse of the wooden horse. The horse is – as Rudolf Steiner explained in the lectures on the Apocalypse – the symbol of intelligence,[1] and intelligence is indeed the soul faculty that has to be developed in the age of the consciousness soul. Yet, unless intelligence is transformed by spiritual knowledge – unless it is 'spiritualised' – it can become a destructive force. The saga contains a warning to this effect: Odysseus sets out on the homeward journey with many companions but in the end he is the only one who survives. The others have fallen by the wayside, some earlier, some later.

The first test they have to pass is the meeting with the Cyclops, giants with one eye in the middle of the forehead. This one eye is the 'third eye', a remnant of atavistic clairvoyant forces. They must first be eliminated, and with them all visionary experiences, all states of trance, all mediumistic 'receiving of messages' so that human beings can develop the clarity of intelligence, and through it a higher conscious activity of that 'lotus flower' in the middle of the forehead. Odysseus outwits the clumsy Cyclops and blinds him. It means that intelligence has freed itself from forces which belong to the past.

Then the sailors come under the spell of the sorceress Circe, who turns some of them into swine. When intelligence is used only to satisfy our low passions and desires, we are no better than swine. Our whole present-day civilisation is under this spell; modern advertising, modern sales techniques, are manifestations of the magic of Circe. Odysseus receives from Hermes a plant which protects him and helps him to break Circe's power. The plant is moderation, a virtue our consumer society has still to learn.

The next threat to intelligence comes from inside the soul – the song of the Sirens, or wishful thinking, indulging in daydreams which arise from our selfish hopes and fears, fantasy-images and illusions which enable us to forget the realities of life. The American humourist James Thurber wrote a short story which became a classic, 'The Secret Life of Walter Mitty'. The man he describes finds consolation for his drab existence by creating a fantasy world in which he is one day a flying ace in World War I, the next time an intrepid explorer, or a society lion, and so on. There is a Walter Mitty in every one of us, though not everybody has his fertile imagination.

It is, in fact, imagination, one of our higher faculties, which leads us astray. This is what is meant by the song of the Sirens. Odysseus closes the ears of his sailors with wax so that they are not tempted by the Sirens, but he lets himself be tied to the mast so that he will hear the Sirens without being overcome by the magic of their song. The sailors with wax in their ears are the people who are protected against the Sirens through lack of imagination. Odysseus hears the song and he has imagination but he is held by self-discipline, inner discipline. This is what is meant by the mast. Where there is this discipline, intelligence is enriched by imagination and not destroyed, as it was in the case of Walter Mitty.

The next danger the voyagers have to face is the encounter with Scylla and Charybdis. Their ship has to pass a narrow strait between a rock on which it would founder (Scylla) and a whirlpool which would suck it down into the depths (Charybdis). Odysseus saves ship and crew by steering a middle course, keeping the same distance from each danger. The rock is Ahriman and the whirlpool Lucifer, and it is by keeping a balance between the two that a human being finds the right way forward. We need fully awake intelligence to keep this balance. It should be noted that, of all the Greek myths, only the saga of Odysseus contains such a clear reference to Ahriman and Lucifer.

Up to this part of the story Odysseus is still accompanied by comrades. Now there comes a decisive change. The sailors kill some cattle sacred to Apollo while Odysseus is asleep. The vengeance of the gods destroys ship and crew and only Odysseus, grasping a wild fig tree growing from a rock, can save himself. The fig tree is the age-old symbol of mystery initiation. On this path of initiation etheric forces used for the physical life of the body must be made to serve a higher purpose – spiritual development. As long as these forces (the cattle sacred to Apollo) are used physically (the eating of the cattle) the soul cannot enter the higher spheres of existence, the spheres of immortality – it remains bound to the mortal body.

This is what is meant by the 'death' of the companions of Odysseus; they cannot follow him to higher spheres of existence. He alone can tread the path of initiation (the fig tree) and use the etheric forces spiritually (sacred to Apollo). On this path the soul is freed from the physical body and enters higher planes.

The first higher region which the soul enters on the path of initiation is the astral world. In the myth this world is represented by the island of the nymph Calypso. Odysseus is made very welcome there but he is not allowed to stay beyond a certain time. He must go on to a higher realm. Above the astral plane is the true spirit-land or devachan represented in the myth by the island of the Phaeacians. The whole description of the hospitality and the life of the people of this island conveys a mood of serenity not found anywhere else in Homer's *Odyssey*. Only someone who was both an initiate and a great poet like Homer could express the nature of the spiritual world in images taken from the sense-world. A higher consciousness than our normal waking awareness is necessary for the experience of the astral world and of devachan. The task of Odysseus is not only to have these higher experiences but to bring the knowledge he has gained from them down to ordinary human consciousness. In the myth this is the 'homecoming' of Odysseus.

We are told that Penelope, the wife of Odysseus, is beleaguered by unwelcome suitors who want to persuade her that her husband has died and to force her to marry one of them. She only keeps them at bay by promising to make her choice when she has finished weaving a large tapestry. She prolongs the task by undoing every night what she has woven during the day. Odysseus, who has been warned by Pallas Athene what to expect, enters his house disguised as a beggar. The suitors make him the butt of their jokes until the beggar gets hold of a bow – it is his own – and then he lets the arrows fly and disposes of the men who have harassed Penelope. At long last Odysseus is reunited with her.

Penelope represents the normal waking consciousness. During the day this consciousness is exposed to the intrusive forces of the sense-world. We develop a sense of reality – what is real and what is not – from these impressions, but every night this sense is lost, dissolved. It is only when the knowledge gained by higher forms of consciousness (imagination, inspiration, intuition) is united with the ordinary consciousness that there arises a sense of *spiritual* reality in the soul. The human being begins to feel itself as a spiritual and not merely a physical being; and then the sense impressions have lost their power over the soul.

The knowledge acquired on the path of initiation appears, at first, to have much less value than any kind of knowledge found in the physical world. It cannot be proved by experiment, it remains forever incomplete, it cannot be imposed on the soul. It depends for its acceptance on a person's good will, just as a beggar depends on other people's good will. Spiritual knowledge must appear in this world as a beggar. This was the reason why this knowledge was in ancient times – even in the times of ancient Greece – kept secret in the mystery centres. The people outside the mysteries would not have appreciated it. The Odysseus myth refers therefore not to the age which created it, but to the future – which is the present in which we live.

The being which turns Odysseus, the bearer of intelligence that has become spiritual knowledge, into a beggar, is Pallas Athene, the goddess of wisdom. She represents the Greek conception of the being we call 'Sophia', the divine wisdom. Just as Christ did not come into the world as a powerful king, so divine wisdom does not come into the world as a ruling queen; it comes in the guise of a beggar. And the suitors who make the beggar the butt of their jokes are the materialistic sciences and philosophies of our time.

10

The Myth of Demeter
and Persephone

In a lecture given in 1904 Rudolf Steiner said:

> It is said that in the Greek mystery schools the future
> was foretold to the people. It was no vague, abstract
> account of what was to happen to man in the future, but
> instructions that would lead him along the pathway to
> the future, and he was shown what he had to do for his
> future development ...
> Sagas ... are derived from the mystery schools, and
> are no less than the representation of what was enacted
> therein as the great drama of human destiny.[1]

Earlier we saw that the Prometheus myth and the Odysseus
myth belong to this category of sagas which refer to stages
of mankind's evolution. Odysseus represents the fifth post-
Atlantean epoch, our own, the age of the consciousness soul.
We can, therefore, expect that the next myth in this chapter
(it is also the last Greek myth) has something to say about the
sixth post-Atlantean epoch, the age when it will be the task of
mankind to develop the spirit-self or manas.

It is the myth of Demeter and Persephone which can lead
to an understanding of the secret of manas. When this higher
member of the human being is mentioned by Rudolf Steiner it
is usually described as the purified or transformed astral body.

When the I has cleansed the astral body of selfish desires
and passions there arises the spirit-self and this means a self
that is selfless. However, when it is not a matter of a brief
indication of the nature of manas but when it is necessary to
reach a deeper understanding, we find that there is still another
aspect mentioned in various lectures. As the astral body is at
present, it needs to be purified if a human being is to make any
spiritual progress, but the human astral forces were not from
the beginning darkened by desires. At first the astral body had
the purity which we now associate with manas, the spirit-self.
Rudolf Steiner described it with the words:

> The astral body was ... illuminated by divine-spiritual
> beings. The astral body was pure and bright, and it
> flowed around what was present as the rudiments of the
> physical and etheric bodies.[2]

This is the key to an understanding of what is meant by
Persephone, the daughter of the gods Zeus and Demeter.
Hades, the god of the underworld, takes her by force into
his dark realm. This is the Greek version of what the Old
Testament calls the Fall of man. It means that the astral body
is drawn deeper into the physical body than was the intention
of the good gods. The physical body is the 'underworld'
which has captured Persephone. In another lecture we are
told that manas descended into human souls in the middle of
the Lemurian epoch of our evolution. Before that time there
existed no desire-principle in the real sense.

> Of this epoch the Bible says: 'The Spirit of God brooded
> over the waters.' The principle of love was not *within* the
> beings, but outside.[3]

When this warmth or love entered into the beings it
became the fire of passions and desires. If we return now to
the Greek myth we find that Demeter takes the form of an old

woman and wanders through the earthly world in search of Persephone. The King of Eleusis takes pity on the old crone and takes her into his household, where she is given the task of looking after the king's baby son. Demeter wants to reward the king's kindness by making his son immortal. To this end she takes the child at night and holds him over a fire. But before the act of divine magic is completed, the queen enters and snatches her baby in horror from the old woman. Now Demeter reveals herself – and at her command Eleusis becomes a mystery centre, the most important in the whole of Greece.

Here the myth describes what the good gods undertake to help mankind while Persephone is held by Hades; they establish mystery centres where human beings can undergo initiation. On this path the soul is purified in the holy fire of self-denial and the overcoming of desire. The process cannot be quite completed, for the same reason that Achilles has a vulnerable heel and Siegfried is vulnerable at a spot between his shoulders – both are initiates of pre-Christian mysteries and until the coming of Christ it was not possible to purify the whole human being. The myth indicates what the purpose of the mysteries was and what Rudolf Steiner expressed in the words:

> Then men had to consider how they could win back
> the pure flow of the astral body, and there arose in the
> Eleusinian mysteries what was known as the search for
> the original purity of the astral body. One aim of the
> Eleusinian mysteries, and also of the Egyptians, was to
> recapture the astral body in its pristine golden flow.[4]

We can see now that Persephone is the astral body as it was in the beginning and as a future ideal for the pupils of the mysteries. But it is also what mankind as a whole has to achieve in the future. The people who sought initiation in the mysteries of Eleusis were not merely striving for some personal spiritual development but were also pioneers anticipating and preparing what *every* human soul will have to experience in the future, the purification of the astral body. And this future is not so terribly far away. It is no further away than the epoch of the spirit-self, or as it is called in the Apocalypse, the age of Philadelphia. In this sense the Demeter-Persephone myth is again a prophetic myth, as was the saga of Odysseus.

But the words used for the spirit-self – purification, overcoming of selfish desires – are too abstract to convey anything of its real nature. One has to take account of another aspect of the mysteries to realise that they did not deal in abstractions or theories. It was the Greek mystery centres, Eleusis in particular, which brought something into the world that had not existed before. At first it was only within the mystery schools that certain myths were acted on a stage. The impact of a dramatised version of a myth is infinitely stronger than a mere telling of a tale. And then the presentation of myths by people acting the parts was brought out of the mystery temples and placed before the ordinary people – the art of drama was born.

But this was not a more or less accidental development. There was a definite purpose behind it and Aristotle – who was not an initiate of the mysteries – was still capable of understanding this purpose. He spoke of drama as designed to rouse fear and compassion and, through these emotions, to bring about the experience of catharsis in the soul. But the fear and compassion a spectator feels at a performance is not concerned with their own person; they temporarily identify themselves with the person whose grief or pain is presented on the stage. They go out of themselves and become one with another being. And this is what the spirit-self means, what manas means: to experience the other person's unhappiness as one's own. And this is 'catharsis', which is simply the Greek word for cleansing or purification. When the soul – or, to be more concrete, the astral body – feels the joys and sorrows of others as its own, it *is* purified, it is cleansed of narrow selfishness, and is no longer the captive of Hades. The art of drama is a means to educate mankind for the spirit-self, a means given to humanity by the Greek mysteries.

We still have to understand the meaning of the end of the Demeter-Persephone myth. There is eventually a compromise between the Olympian (or cosmic) gods and Hades, the lord of the underworld: Persephone will spend two thirds of the year with her kinsfolk, the cosmic gods, but she has to dwell for one third of the year in the dark kingdom of Hades. She ate the fruit of the pomegranate tree while she was in the underworld and this compels her to come back to Hades again and again.

We can only *begin* to develop manas during the Earth phase of evolution. Not Earth but Jupiter, the next phase, is the stage when the spirit-self will be for humanity what the I is now. For the whole of the Earth phase the transformation of the astral body cannot be complete. And our impure desires are subject to the law of karma, which compels us to incarnate in physical bodies. The eating of the pomegranate is the symbol for this necessity.

Persephone, the soul, must therefore alternate between a life in the spiritual world after death and life in the physical body after birth. But this great cosmic rhythm is reflected during life on earth in a much shorter rhythm: sleeping and waking. In sleep too, the astral body, together with the I, is freed from the physical body and then returns to it when we awake. And because the human being is not – as materialistic science tells us – an insignificant creature, a mere accident of evolution, but the centre of evolution of the earth, the earth itself is subject to the same rhythm of awakening and falling asleep. This is the rhythm of the seasons of the year.

The mysteries of Eleusis (one could call them the Persephone mysteries) taught their pupils to look upon autumn as a time when, together with the death of the plant world, there is an awakening of the earth-spirit – as it is in a human being when waking up in the morning. But in spring the earth-spirit goes out into the cosmos, as a human being's soul does in falling asleep, and this is accompanied by a rebirth of life in nature. And thus there were two festivals celebrated in Eleusis, one in the early spring and one in the autumn.

But the pupils of the Eleusinian mysteries were told that as the earth goes through sleep and awakening, so your soul goes through death and rebirth and gradually in the course of incarnations becomes purified until it shines with the pure golden light it had in the beginning. Then the soul has become Persephone – the spirit-self.

11

The Egyptian Mysteries

In *Christianity as Mystical Fact* the chapter on the mystery wisdom of Egypt follows the one on Greek mythology. This is rather surprising since one would expect the older civilisation to be discussed before the later one. The reason for this disregard of chronological sequence lies in the profound 'Osiris' concept of ancient Egypt. It is this concept which opens the way to introduce for the first time in this book the figure of Jesus and thus to approach the Mystery of Golgotha.

None of the divinities or heroes of Greece could provide a concept leading to the very core of Christianity in so far as it is a 'mystical fact'. And so this chapter, which forms the middle of the book, has to take as its start the theme of Osiris, a being who is far more difficult to understand than Zeus or Apollo.

To find the meaning of Osiris one has to consider the Egyptian civilisation as a whole. From the point of view of our time, it would seem that the ancient Egyptians were obsessed with the idea of death, or rather, of existence after death. No sooner had a Pharaoh come to the throne than he began to prepare his tomb, his coffin, the treasures to be buried with him and the paintings on the walls of the tomb. Among the treasures there would be the *Book of the Dead*, an itinerary of the soul's sojourn in the spiritual world. And in this concern with life after death the Pharaoh only reflected the attitude of the whole nation.

What lies behind this preoccupation with the world beyond the grave is that the Egyptians expected something, a certain experience which could not be found here on earth but would come to them after death. Yet it was understood that this experience was essential to become a complete human being. So for the Egyptians, the possibility to feel fully and truly human existed only after death. And this 'something' which they hoped to find in the life hereafter, this something which was necessary to become fully human, was the I-consciousness.

At the time of the Egyptian civilisation people felt themselves as members of a national or tribal group-soul and not as separate individuals. It was a kind of existence similar – although on a higher level – to life in the animal kingdom. And where human beings have a strong group-soul experience there is also a certain feeling of kinship with animals, as can be seen from the animal totems in tribal societies. The animal-headed gods of Egypt are an expression of the same instinctive feeling that they, like the lions or eagles, were members of a group-soul.

But at the same time Egyptians felt the question: 'What is it that raises me above the animals – what is it that makes me human?' And from the mystery temples of Egypt came the answer to this question: 'You can only become conscious of that which makes you human when you have left the physical body. It is Osiris.' For Egyptians, I-consciousness could not arise during life on earth but was given after death. This was expressed by saying, 'Here on earth your name is Imhotep. After death you will become Osiris Imhotep.'

The Egyptian *Book of the Dead* speaks of the higher members of the human being just as we do in anthroposophy. It speaks of the Ka, which is the etheric body, and of the Ba, which is the astral body. It describes how the soul, the Ba, is brought to the Hall of Judgement, where the heart of that person is weighed on a pair of scales in the presence of the supreme judge, Osiris. And if the good nature of the heart outweighs the evil, the soul is accepted by Osiris, it becomes Osiris – or, as we would express it, it becomes conscious of the I.

About 1350 BC a Pharaoh came to the throne who foresaw a time when the human being would awaken to the

I-consciousness during life on earth and that this would be due to the Sun Spirit, Aton. This prophetic spirit was the Pharaoh Akhenaton. But after his death the priests of the decadent Ammon religion tried to destroy every vestige of the cult of Aton.

A few generations after Akhenaton, the Osiris mystery was taken away from Egypt and given to another people, the Jews. This was the task of Moses. The spirit whom the Egyptians called Osiris, spoke to Moses out of the burning thorn-bush and said 'I am the I am' – thus declaring himself as the spirit of I-consciousness. As Rudolf Steiner explained in a lecture, Osiris is the same being as Yahweh, a Moon-spirit.[1] In the Jewish religion, what Egyptians could only find in life after death came into *earthly* life. It was still bound up with hereditary forces and limited to the descendants of Abraham, but it was no longer something that could only be found when the soul had left the physical body.

At this point it becomes necessary to ask why the I-consciousness meant so much to the Egyptians that they looked forward to receiving it in the hereafter – or why it meant so much to the Jews that they regarded themselves as a 'chosen people' in whom it awakened as a gift of Yahweh in life on earth. The answer to this question appears already in the Egyptian *Book of the Dead*. As mentioned before, the soul meets Osiris in the Hall of Judgement. It is Osiris who pronounces judgement upon what is good or evil in the soul before him. It is Osiris, the I-consciousness, who is the supreme judge as to what is right or wrong, good or evil.

Ancient Egyptians could not find a moral incentive or a moral law within themselves during life on earth. The moral principles which ruled the life of the individual and the community were laid down by the priests who, as initiates of the Osiris mysteries, had received their inspiration from Osiris. The voice which spoke to the Egyptian initiates when their bodies were in a trance-like state, spoke to Moses on Mount Sinai and gave him the Ten Commandments.

In fact, what was given to the Jews was a whole system of laws which regulated every detail of life. Not the individual, but the Law of Moses decided what was right or wrong, good or evil. Not the individual, but the Jews as a nation had an I-consciousness. The moral law which springs from the soul of the individual was proclaimed for the first time when the words were spoken, 'I AM the Way and the Truth and the Life.'

At the time of the Mystery of Golgotha the Pharisees, who were the most faithful adherents of the laws of Moses, could only regard the teaching of Jesus as blasphemy. Yet it was a Pharisee, Saul, when he had become Paul, who was the first to recognise that Christ had freed mankind from any moral law imposed from outside. The judge, the 'Osiris', was present in every human individual. This has been a spiritual reality ever since the Mystery of Golgotha, but it took almost two thousand years before this reality could become a conscious experience for all people on earth. At the end of the nineteenth century mankind was ready for 'ethical individualism', as Rudolf Steiner called it in his book *The Philosophy of Freedom*. The first part of this book, the theory of knowledge, opens the way to the Isis mysteries. The second part, the ethical individualism, is the modern equivalent of the Osiris mysteries. With *The Philosophy of Freedom*, the *Book of the Dead* of ancient Egypt has become the *Book of the Living*.

There is still another mystery secret connected with Osiris. Rudolf Steiner refers to it in a passage in this chapter of *Christianity as Mystical Fact* which is difficult to grasp in German and quite obscure in any translation. The following is an attempt to render the meaning in English without adhering to a word-by-word translation:

> Between being human and being a god there is only a difference of degree and a difference of number. What we meet here is, fundamentally, the mystery concept of the secret of 'number' (which means the secret of the 'one' and the 'many'). Osiris as a cosmic being is one;

yet he is present as the undivided one in each of the
many – that is in each human soul. Every human soul
is an Osiris, yet there is also the 'one' Osiris as a being
on his own. Human beings evolve towards Osiris and
their becoming a god lies at the end of this evolution.
If one takes this view of humanity and of God one sees
divinity as a potential to be developed rather than as a
state of being.[2]

The statement contained in this passage that between a
human being and God there is only a difference of degree
is also the key to the words of the Psalm that Christ quoted,
'You are gods.'[3] The divine is already present in a human
being in the same way as the full human potential is already
present in a baby. The beings which we call gods have already
fully developed what, in us, is still at an immature stage,
but it is there – we are gods in the same sense as the baby
is human. If this is understood one will also find another
statement justified which occurs earlier than the above passage
of *Christianity as Mystical Fact*: if the human being is a still
imperfect god, God is nothing else but a perfect human being.
All this is implied in the Osiris concept of ancient Egypt and
we can now understand why Rudolf Steiner uses this concept
as an introduction to the Christ concept which speaks of a god
who became human.

There is still another difference between the human being
and God mentioned in the passage quoted before, the one
and the many – the one god who is present in each of the
many human beings. Here it is necessary to consider our
use of the personal pronoun 'I'. We all use the same word
but mean by it something different, something unique – our
own selves. There is only one word, as if it meant the same
for all and each of us – but it does not, it means something
different in every case. Through habit we are not aware of the
paradox in our use of the little word 'I', but it is a paradox.
One could say that, paradox or not, it is only a form of words.

But behind this form of words there is a spiritual reality – the 'one' who is present in the many, in each of us, and who is different in each of us and is yet the same. This is what St Paul expressed in the words 'Not I, but the Christ within me.'

Christ is the only being who can enter the human I. The group-souls of nations or tribes work towards conformity, towards certain characteristics which all members of the group will have in common. Christ – as the group-spirit of all mankind – works in the human I in the direction of making it truly unique, so that it can make its own unique contribution to the evolution of mankind as a whole. And it is Christ himself who weaves all the many different strands into a harmonious whole. Not conformity, but diversity, is the aim of the spirit in whom all 'I's are one and who is one in all the 'I's.

The ancient Egyptians could find a foreshadowing of this experience through Osiris, the Moon god, after death. Between man and that experience lay the abyss of death. If man was to have this experience during life on earth, the abyss of death had to be crossed from the other side – the Sun Spirit had to become human and suffer death on Golgotha.

12

Osiris Initiates

Egyptians looked forward to life after death, when they would find the god Osiris and – if they were good – would themselves become Osiris. But there was another possibility for the Osiris experience: the path of initiation in the mysteries. This path consisted of several stages involving severe trials and tests. At the ultimate stage the seeker of initiation, or neophyte, was put into a condition of near death. In this condition the soul was freed from the body as it is otherwise only in real death. And then it was possible for the soul to experience the meeting with Osiris and becoming Osiris. After three days the soul was brought back into the body by the priests officiating at this ritual. Then this person was an Osiris living in a physical body. This is what it meant to be an initiate – someone who had become an Osiris while still living in a physical body here on earth.

This ultimate stage of initiation was not something just anybody could attain or even aim for. The gods themselves sent the souls chosen to become initiates to earth, and the lives of these souls – long before they were ready for initiation, from the very beginning – showed a certain 'pattern' which marked them as being destined to become initiates. The ordinary people would not realise the significance of certain events in the lives of these children, but the people who were wise in mystery knowledge could and did recognise the signs which heralded the coming of a soul who was to become an initiate.

In this chapter on Egyptian mystery wisdom Rudolf Steiner draws attention to certain features which are common to the story of Buddha and the story of Jesus. They are common because they had in one respect a common destiny: the destiny of initiation. What is however most significant about these two personalities, and a very special feature they had in common, is that although it was their destiny to become initiates, neither Buddha nor Jesus received initiation through the agency of any priesthood or in connection with any mystery centre. The reasons for this are not difficult to discern. At their time the spiritual stream which had flowed through the mystery temples had already dried up. And even though there were still initiates living at that time, none of them would have been worthy or capable of acting as a spiritual teacher or guide to such souls as lived in Gautama Buddha and in Jesus of Nazareth. Yet, if they were destined to become initiates, how could this come about without the institutions which knew and understood the principles of initiation? It came about because for Buddha as well as for Jesus their life on earth was itself a process of initiation.

In the mystery temples initiation was a process which took place in seclusion, removed from the ordinary conditions of life. Buddha, the son of a king, and even more so Jesus, the son of a carpenter, lived their initiation outside the protective shell of a temple and while remaining in touch with the ordinary life of their time. The fact that their lives were their initiation gives the episodes which these lives had in common a special significance. This is the reason why Rudolf Steiner devotes such a large part of this chapter to pointing out these parallels. There would be no point in dwelling on events of a similar nature in both lives if they were not related to the central theme of this chapter and the whole book – initiation.

To understand what this relationship is, one has to be quite clear that initiation is purely a matter of activities in the soul and spirit of a human being. Outer factors such as instructions or taking part in a ritual can have a certain influence, but what really matters is one's own activity on a purely mental, or spiritual, level. How can one describe such subtle processes? For our time it is necessary to speak of them in the form of concepts, which is what Rudolf Steiner has done. This was not possible in ancient times, and when the mystery priests wanted to tell their pupils what inner experiences had to occur in their souls, they did so in the form of pictures, of images. It was fully understood by the pupils that the images used were *not* the reality, they only indicated or hinted at the reality.

Buddha and Christ received no such instructions in the form of imaginations. What happened in their case was that the images of the mystery priests became real events in their lives. Yet even though the events were real enough in the sense-world, they were still no more than symbols for the spiritual reality which had to be experienced in the souls of Buddha and Jesus. Instead of having instructors, life itself produced situations which were similar to the images used by the temple priests. But like the images, the life-situations were symbols for a reality within their souls. This is how the similar episodes in the lives of Buddha and Jesus have to be understood; although they were quite real to all concerned, they were at the same time symbolic images of the realities one has to find in soul and spirit on the path of initiation.

The first feature the stories have in common is an annunciation. Both mothers receive a message from the spiritual world that the child they expect has a great mission. What corresponds to this message in the inner life of a soul on the path of initiation? The soul feels that there is to be born in it a higher being – its own immortal spirit. It *is* a kind of birth when the spirit awakens in a human being. This is the reason why the initiates were called 'twice born'.

The next event is that there are wise men who recognise in the child a superior being. This too corresponds to an inner experience. The soul has already, before the awakening of the spirit, developed certain faculties. They are the result of the long evolution of mankind. That we have a language to communicate, even that we have thinking, feeling and will, are gifts due to an ancient wisdom which guided mankind. But when the spirit awakens, all the faculties one has had before recognise the higher light which begins to shine in the soul.

The third episode speaks of a man who, as an individual, recognises and praises the infant who will bring salvation. This man is a symbol for all that which the soul has achieved through its own efforts before initiation. Whatever this achievement may be in the eyes of the world or even in the soul's own estimation, it is meaningless and worthless unless it can be connected with the spirit that is born in the soul.

Then follows an occasion when each of the boys is separated from his parents, who have to search for them until the children are eventually found and reunited with their families. This is an image of an important step on the path of initiation. Through the awakening of the spirit, the soul becomes estranged from the ties of blood – family, nation, race – it becomes 'homeless'. This is, however, a temporary condition because it is the wisdom of karma which has placed the soul in a particular family and nationality. And so the soul has to gain a new, conscious relationship to the karmic environment of family, nation and race.

At the 'homeless' stage, the soul is already penetrating into the region of unconscious instincts. It has to descend even deeper into this region at the next step. That step is symbolised in the legends of Buddha and Jesus by a woman who gives praise to the child and the mother who gave it birth. The woman represents the unconscious wisdom in the human being's nature, a wisdom greater than all our conscious knowledge. On the path of initiation the light of the awakened spirit begins to shine in the region of the instincts and gradually the unconscious wisdom becomes conscious understanding.

By entering the region of the unconscious, the soul is challenging the forces which have the power to lead the human being astray as long as they can influence him through unconscious urges and desires. And so the soul has to confront Lucifer and Ahriman. This is the counterpart of the stories of temptation in the lives of Buddha and Jesus.

The seventh stage is a kind of culmination – in the lives of the two holy men it is called 'transfiguration'. Their disciples saw them shining with a great light. This corresponds on the path of initiation to the fullness of the inner light; it has grown so strong that it even illuminates sleep. The soul can be awake even when the body is asleep. But, as Rudolf Steiner points out, from here onwards the stories of Buddha and Jesus differ. Buddha can go as far as the transfiguration, not further. Jesus goes on to death and resurrection.

In the mystery temples of Egypt, the neophyte was put into a death-like condition by a group of priests. And it was again this group which brought them back to life after three days. No individual could perform this ultimate act of initiation for himself. Even a soul as advanced as Buddha, who had passed through all the other steps of initiation by his own spiritual strength, did not venture into the realm of death. It needed the power of Christ to overcome death.

But with the death and resurrection of Jesus Christ we come also to a reversal of the roles of symbol and reality concerning initiation. For all previous stages we had to regard the events in the lives of Buddha and Jesus as symbols. The reality which these symbols indicated was in the inner soul-processes they experienced. But it is the other way round with death and resurrection. The death-like condition of the neophyte in the mysteries was not a real death. It was a deep coma, but not actual death, and it was therefore only a symbolic death. But what Christ suffered was not a symbolic condition, it was real death. The mystery-death was a symbol, but the crucifixion and resurrection were realities. And because the latter were real they made the symbolic death of the mystery temples obsolete and superfluous. Since the Mystery of Golgotha human beings have to seek initiation through the living Christ who has gone through death for all human souls.

This makes it understandable that with the Mystery of Golgotha all pre-Christian mysteries had come to an end. Although some mystery cults existed for several centuries into the Christian era, they had become a form without content and would have withered away even if the adherents of the new Christian religion had not attacked and destroyed the mystery temples and their wisdom. It was a tragic mistake that those who understood the ancient mysteries, like Julian the Apostate, did not recognise Christ as the fulfilment of these mysteries. It was equally tragic that, as the result of a deliberate policy engineered from Rome, early Christians were misled and prevented from recognising in the mysteries a preparation for the coming of Christ.

There *were* people who had a deeper understanding, and who knew the connection between the mysteries and Christianity, but they were few in number and what they knew had to be kept as secret as the ancient mystery knowledge. Their secret was that a new initiation had come into the world – initiation through Christ. It is strange to think that it took almost two thousand years before this could be said openly and publicly by Rudolf Steiner.

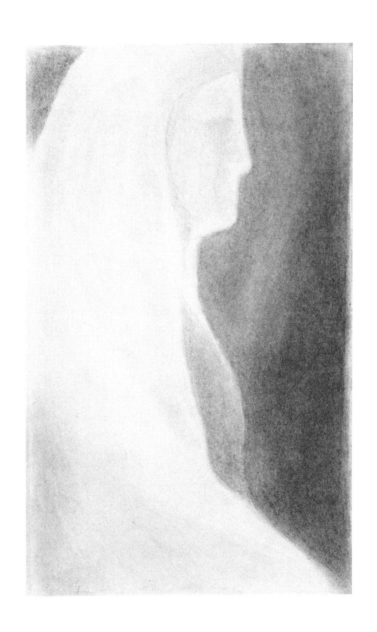

Isis

The Sun Spirit

The Moon Goddess

The Annunciation of Jesus

The Conception of Jesus

Lucifer and Ahriman

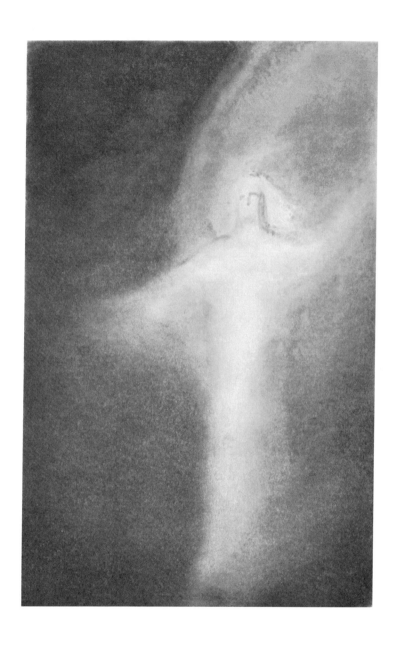

The Guardian of the Threshold

Persephone between Demeter and Hades

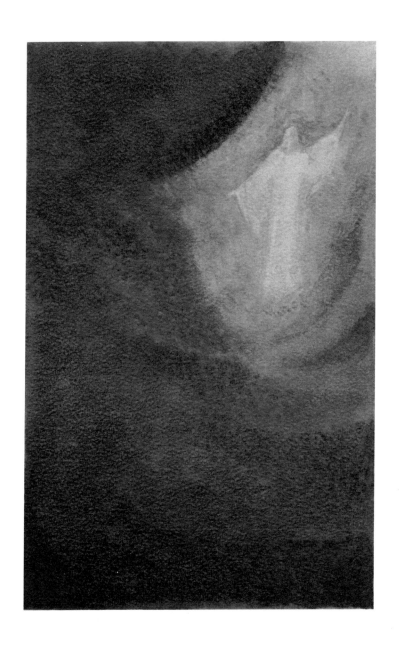

The Bath-Kol

Adam Kadmon

The Child Jesus

The Path

Dawn

The Young Jesus

Anthroposophia

The Risen Christ

13

Events in the Gospels

The next chapter of *Christianity as Mystical Fact,* headed 'The Gospels', takes up a theme which has already appeared in the previous one. We saw that certain events which appear in the life stories of both Buddha and Jesus have to be understood as symbolic images for inner experiences on the path of initiation. Now we have to add to this interpretation the concept that it does not really matter whether such events actually happened as they are told or even whether they happened at all on the physical plane. It is a concept which is just as difficult to accept for the unbeliever as for the believing Christian; both will only accept physical facts as a reality. But this was not the attitude of the writers of the four gospels; they had no intention of recording the physical facts of a biography of Jesus. What they wanted to describe was the life of someone in whom the divine spirit was fully awakened, the life of an initiate who was, for them, *the* initiate, for with him began the initiation of all mankind.

Since each of the authors of the gospels was connected with a different mystery tradition, their views of the ideal great initiate varied, and so did the pictures they drew in their respective gospels. This explanation given by Rudolf Steiner for the numerous disagreements between the gospels creates quite a problem for the modern mind. Which events recounted in the gospels can we trust to be physical facts and which have to be regarded as 'only' symbolic representations of a particular path of initiation? The answer is that really and truly it does not matter, for the distinction between physical and spiritual reality has no meaning in relation to the Christ Jesus. He is real and it is his reality we have to find through the images and words of the gospels. Whether a particular event described in any of the gospels happened physically, or has to be understood as a symbolic representation of a spiritual reality, is altogether irrelevant.

This becomes quite clear from the example given by Rudolf Steiner in this chapter. He draws attention to an event which is recorded in the Gospel of Mark as something which had actually happened: Jesus was disappointed at finding no fruit on a fig tree and cursed the tree. In the Gospel of Luke the story appears as a parable which Jesus tells the disciples – a farmer finds that a fig tree has not borne fruit for several years and gives orders that the tree be cut down. Rudolf Steiner makes no attempt to satisfy our curiosity as to which of the two Gospels – as we would say – 'got it right'. He also leaves it to the reader to ponder about the meaning of this story. After all, it seems rather strange that Jesus should get so bad-tempered about a fruitless tree that he would curse the innocent plant.

As a matter of fact, the example chosen by Rudolf Steiner is very apt, because it refers to the main subject of the first half of the book. The fig tree is the symbol of the mystery initiation. There is another event described in the gospels which remains obscure if the meaning of the fig tree is not understood. Jesus says to Nathanael 'I saw you under the fig tree' and the man responds by calling him a 'Master' – that means a high initiate. Otherwise Jesus could not have known that the man was on the path of initiation.

In the Odysseus myth we have come across the same symbol. The sailors have aroused the anger of the gods and their ship founders in a storm. Only Odysseus is saved. The waves throw him against a rock on which a fig tree grows and he gets hold of a root of that tree and so escapes from death. Here too the fig tree represents initiation, which makes Odysseus conscious of that in him which is immortal and not subject to death. But it is just this initiation which is made obsolete by the coming of Christ. In fact it was already in decadence at the time of the Mystery of Golgotha and this is what is meant by saying that the fig tree does not bear any more fruit. This is what both gospels, Mark and Luke, want to convey. And what they also convey – although indirectly – is that henceforth there can only be initiation through the Christ-impulse. Anything else can only be evil and is cursed.

One can see that Rudolf Steiner had a very good reason for bringing in the story of the fig tree at this juncture of the book. What is not at all clear is why the fig tree was the symbol for the old mystery initiation – this is in itself a kind of mystery. And in order to find the reason for the choice of this symbol one has to ask, what were the forces by means of which one could become an initiate in the ancient mysteries? They could only be forces which exist in the human being naturally, whether entering on the path of initiation or not. And as long as they are not used for spiritual development they have other functions in the human organism – they are the forces of reproduction. The mystery pupils were told that human reproduction had become what it is through the Fall of man.

Before the Fall – and before the division of the sexes which came through it – the human reproductive organs were of a plant-like nature. And the leaves of the fig tree are in their form nearest to the form of the human reproductive organs before the Fall. Something of this mystery tradition reached the outside world and gave rise to the strange custom of covering the genitals of statues with fig leaves. But the mystery pupils were told that through the meditative exercises they had to practise, the original pure spiritual forces, which humanity had before birth and death came into the world, could be regained. This was also the reason why – at least for the higher stages of initiation – pupils had to be celibate. The mysteries of pre-Christian times could only lead pupils to the spirit by going back, by seeking a condition which had once existed in the past. This is what the symbol of the fig tree stood for, a path of initiation which led to the past.

Christ brought the impulse of a new love which has nothing to do with sex and which leads into the future. And this meant that the fig tree could no more bear fruit and was cursed.

There was, however, one kind of initiation in pre-Christian times which did not look backwards but forwards, and the initiates of that particular mystery centre were called by a name which indicates that they were looking towards the future: they were called 'prophets'. Moses, Elijah, Jonah, Daniel and all the other prophets named in the Old Testament were the initiates of Israel. But this particular feature of Jewish history has to be understood in a wider context.

As we have seen, the lives of individualities such as Buddha or Jesus followed a certain pattern, the pattern of the stages of initiation. Their life was at the same time their initiation. In the same way the history of the Jews, from Abraham to the Mystery of Golgotha, is also an initiation, the initiation of a whole people. The Mystery of Golgotha could not have taken place unless it had been prepared through many generations and this preparation involved the Jewish people as a whole.

The Old Testament is for the most part nothing else but the history of the Jews, a history which has heroes, saints and villains, triumphs and disasters, like the history of any other nation in the world. But no other nation has ever regarded their history or the record of that history as something holy. Yet the Jewish history that Christians call the Old Testament is regarded as a holy book, not only by Jews but also by Christianity. And what lies behind the strange fact that the history of an insignificant Middle-Eastern tribe is treated as Holy Writ is this. It really is a holy story, the story of an initiation, the initiation of a whole nation. And the people who knew the secret, that the history of the Jews was to follow the pattern of an initiation, were the prophets. This is the reason why they often seem fanatical in their condemnation of any deviation from the laws of Moses. The rigid discipline imposed on the neophyte in the mystery temples had to be borne for centuries by a whole people – and the prophets were the guardians of that discipline.

The incidents of Jewish history appear in a different light if they are seen in the context of initiation. One reads in the Old Testament that the Jews were for a time in exile in Egypt, and later they were again in exile in Babylon. But, as we have seen, Egypt cultivated especially the mysteries of life after death. The Babylonians, the founders of astrology, had a profound understanding of the mysteries of life before birth. Although in Egypt only Moses was an initiate of the Osiris mysteries and in Babylon only Daniel was an initiate of the star wisdom, the Jewish people as a whole had to experience the spiritual atmosphere of these two mystery streams. These exiles were necessary parts of the initiation of the Israelites.

Another important stage in this initiation of a whole people was the building of Solomon's temple in Jerusalem. The proportions of the temple were the proportions of the human body, and details like the two pillars Jachin and Boaz or the inner sanctuary, the Holy of Holies, corresponded to spiritual facts in the human organisation. The House of Yahweh was an anticipation of and preparation for the 'house' that would be offered to the God who was to become man, the body of Jesus. And the events connected with the building of this temple became themselves an initiation mystery which has continued right into the present in the initiation rituals of the masonic lodges. Although this 'initiation' is today no more than a formality, it is the remnant of a great spiritual tradition and this tradition rests upon the events surrounding the building of Solomon's temple.

When Rudolf Steiner refers to the Jewish mystery tradition this is not merely a reminder of the Jewish background to the Mystery of Golgotha, this reference points to a direct connection between the Jewish mysteries and the Christ event. When, at the baptism in the River Jordan, Christ entered into the being of Jesus, the initiation of the Jews as a whole had reached its fulfilment. It had also come to an end.

In the lecture series *The Fifth Gospel,* Rudolf Steiner speaks of the Bath-Kol, the voice which had spoken to the Jewish prophets, the initiates of Israel, and had inspired them.[1] Jesus was the last man to whom it was given to hear that voice. It was this Bath-Kol which pronounced to him the lines which – in reverse order – Christ gave to the world as the Lord's Prayer. What we have in this prayer is the last gift of the powers which once lived in the Jewish mystery-initiation.

14

The Awakening of Lazarus

The next chapter of *Christianity as Mystical Fact* deals with the awakening of Lazarus, an event about which Rudolf Steiner spoke in greater detail in later years when he gave the lectures on the Gospel of John. However, much of what is said in his book is fundamental and is not repeated anywhere else.

We have to keep in mind that the special concern of this book is to establish that there is a link between the ancient mysteries and Christianity. Yet all we have read so far could only serve to demonstrate that among the early Christians – and particularly among the writers of the gospels – there existed a knowledge of mystery traditions and that they regarded the life of Christ in the light of this knowledge. But this does not prove beyond any doubt that what Christ gave to mankind was, in point of fact, related to the mysteries. The authors of the gospels may interpret his words and deeds in this way, but was it really so? There is only one event which answers this question positively and that is the awakening of Lazarus.

No one has ever, before Rudolf Steiner, interpreted the Lazarus event as an act of initiation – and no one could have done so because no one had sufficient knowledge of the ancient mysteries and what went on there. Yet, once Rudolf Steiner has given the key to this event, it seems so obvious that Jesus performed an initiation rite that one wonders why the idea did not occur to anyone else. But Rudolf Steiner does more than merely point out that the 'illness' of Lazarus is the death-like sleep of the mystery initiation and that the awakening call

'Lazarus, come forth' is part of the mystery tradition. The whole event is placed in a certain context. It is related to the first words of the Gospel of John: 'In the beginning was the Word. And the Word was with God. And the Word was a God.' What is meant by 'the Word' as designation of a divine being is certainly far removed from the words of our everyday language. In order to come to some understanding of the divine Word or 'Logos' we have to realise that everything in the human being is in a process of evolution and that the forces we are at present using for speech, for producing words, will also become something else in the course of time.

In a distant future, human reproduction as we know it will come to an end. And then the larynx, our present speech organ, will become the organ of reproduction.[1] Obviously, this will not be a physical, but an etheric organ and the bodies produced by it will be of a much finer substance than our present physical forms, but what matters is this: that the forces we use at present to form words will become forces of reproduction. As the seed of the future plant is hidden in the present one, so there is hidden in the words we speak now the future power of reproduction – and this is a creative power. Reproduction is still only one stage in its development and further, higher stages are to follow. Ultimately it reveals itself as *the* creative power in the world and this is what the Gospel of John means by the Logos.

This creative aspect of the Logos implies also something else. True 'creation' means to produce something new, something which has not been here before. And thus it means a *beginning*. What comes into the world through the Logos is always a new beginning. This is also conveyed by the other name of the Logos, the Son of God. Compared with the Father, the Son represents something new. And because the Logos, the Son of God, brings into the world what is new, what is a beginning, the Gospel of John can proclaim 'In the beginning was the Logos.'

And this brings us to the somewhat startling sentence we find in Steiner's chapter, a sentence which is a purely rhetorical question: 'What would be special about a person raised from the dead if he were, after the resurrection, the same kind of person as he was before his death?' Rudolf Steiner refers to the awakening of Lazarus and, obviously, wants to say that there would be nothing remarkable about Lazarus if he had been the same kind of man after Christ called him from the grave as he had been before. But he *had* been changed and it was a change wrought by the Logos – a change which was a new beginning.

If Lazarus had been initiated in ancient Egypt, the priest performing the ritual would have freed his soul to seek Osiris in the spiritual world – to 'become Osiris' as human souls became Osiris after death; and then the priest would have called him back to earthly existence. And a person initiated in this way was indeed changed, for he had become aware of the Osiris within himself. But what took place in Bethany was not an Egyptian initiation. In this case the power of which Osiris had been a reflection itself performed the initiation rite. And the spirit whom Lazarus met during his death-like sleep when the soul was outside the body, that same spirit was he who stood before the grave and spoke the words 'Lazarus, come forth.' It was an event which, seen from outside, took the form of the age-old mystery initiation. But in reality it was something quite new: the initiation through the forces Christ has given to the human I, the creative forces of the Logos.

There is still another side to the mystery of the Word. A word of our ordinary speech has a meaning. We hear the sounds of a foreign language just as well as the native speaker of that language, but we cannot grasp the meaning of these sounds until we have mastered the language. In the same way, everything we encounter in the world of the senses 'speaks', has something to say, but we do not understand it unless and until we have learned the language of nature. Rudolf Steiner gave special lessons to teach us this language in the lectures *Harmony of the Creative Word,* whose full title in German is 'the human being as the symphonic harmony of the cosmic Word'. It is the cosmic Word, the Logos, which speaks to us through the beings and forces of nature.

But the great difference between human words and the cosmic Word is this: the words of human language *have* meaning while the cosmic Word *gives* meaning. And nothing has any meaning at all except through the Logos. Even Lucifer and Ahriman – great spiritual beings though they are – would have an existence without any meaning if Christ, the Logos, were not in the world. And the whole world would have no meaning without Christ. This is the reason why a materialistic science can only come to a picture of the world which shows the universe and all that is in it as an absurdity without meaning or purpose. And it is true that without Christ, without the Logos, there is no meaning in the universe or in the creatures which inhabit it. The Logos is not only the beginning of the world, but also its meaning.

But what is the meaning and purpose of human existence? Animals do not need a reason for being what they are and doing what they are doing; they are guided by their instincts. For human beings too there once existed an instinctive guidance which gave the soul the assurance that there was a meaning in life on earth. When this instinctive assurance faded away, only the initiates of the mysteries had the possibility to know and to understand the answer to the riddle of human existence. The answer which the initiates found – not as a theory, not as a philosophic concept but as a blazing reality – was: the purpose of man's existence is to become God.

One can understand that the mysteries kept this knowledge secret. Most people would have regarded such an idea as madness and would not have treated it as sacred knowledge. And those who accepted the idea of their own divinity were in danger of being driven into madness. This danger was very real. Rudolf Steiner gives the example of Roman Caesars – Caligula, Nero – who forced the priests to initiate them without the safeguards laid down by the mystery tradition, without the process of purification.[2] And so these emperors came to the real, living experience of their own divinity. That is why they then insisted that they be worshipped as gods in temples built for them.

But of course, as a result of their experiences and as their lives show, they were stark staring mad. Without Christ, the words 'You are gods' can only be taken as madness – or they can drive people mad. Yet, these are the very words Christ spoke.

Christ has come to give the secret of the mysteries to all humanity. And he himself is the safeguard, the protection the human being needs on the path to divinity, which is the path of initiation. And the first person to be thus initiated was Lazarus. As we know from other lectures given by Rudolf Steiner, he is John, the disciple whom Jesus loved and who is the author of the John Gospel.

One may perhaps wonder why this book – the first book in which Rudolf Steiner speaks of the Christ event – considers this event only from the aspect of initiation. Most people have never even heard of initiation, and even among anthroposophists who are familiar with this idea, the majority have no inclination to seek the initiation experience. So why did Rudolf Steiner devote this fundamental book to an aspect of the Mystery of Golgotha which can concern only very few people? Because the purpose of human existence *is* to become gods, and the path to the realisation of the god in us is the path of initiation. And Christ, the god, became human for the very purpose of helping human beings to become god. All the other aspects of the Mystery of Golgotha are part of this main purpose.

15

The Initiation of Mankind

In the chapter about the gospels Rudolf Steiner speaks of the mystery tradition of the Jews contained in the Kabbala. He quotes a saying from this tradition that four rabbis entered upon the secret path to the divine, that one of them died, the second went mad, the third caused terrible devastation and only the fourth entered in peace and returned in peace. The quotation contains a warning that the process of initiation is not without dangers, and the price one has to pay for failure is far higher than any of the disadvantages which follow from failure in some ordinary pursuit.

In a lecture of the Esoteric School Rudolf Steiner said that in ordinary life we are protected against the most dangerous Luciferic influences by the good gods who have given us a strong force to resist these influences.[1] But someone who strives on the esoteric path is using this same force for his spiritual development and so must create his own protection against Lucifer – otherwise he is in greater spiritual danger than is normal for human beings. So there are certain dangers for the individual who seeks the path of initiation. But as we have seen in a previous chapter there is the example of the Jews, whose history up to the Mystery of Golgotha is the story of the initiation of a whole nation. And the history of the Jews after the Mystery of Golgotha is a demonstration of the price of failure on the path of initiation. The legend of Ahasuerus, the Wandering Jew who cannot die, is an image of the consequences of this failure.

It may seem a great injustice that souls who, as individuals, may have had no wish for initiation should have become involved in a group-initiation, that they should have been subject to the severe tests and trials which are inseparable from initiation and that, finally, those who had failed had to pay the price of failure. But we can compare this situation with another quite frequent one. There is a war between two nations. The people who lose their lives in this war may not have wanted the conflict; they may, as individuals, have nothing to do with the cause of the war, but they still become involved, and suffer through their involvement. In both cases, the individual karma is subordinated to a higher cause: the karma of a nation or, in the case of the Jews, the karma of mankind, which made it necessary that the descendants of Abraham, as a group, were made to go through an initiation process. And we can also be certain that the individual soul, having suffered for a higher cause, is enriched by the experience. There *is* a group-karma and since 'no man is an island' we are all involved in the destiny of the groups to which we belong in any incarnation.

But there is one group-karma in which every human soul is involved in every incarnation, from the beginning of Earth phase of evolution to its end: the karma of mankind. And what is the karma of mankind? It is initiation. We can see this from the fact that the stages of the Rosicrucian initiation – imagination, inspiration, intuition – are also the types of consciousness all human beings will develop during the Jupiter, Venus and Vulcan phases of evolution. The Rosicrucian initiation of the individual is an anticipation of the initiation of mankind as a whole. And the individuality chosen to reveal to mankind its destiny, the destiny of initiation, could not be anyone else but the individuality who had been initiated by Christ himself – Lazarus-John. It was John who wrote the Book of Revelation, the Apocalypse. And so there is an inner necessity that the chapter dealing with the awakening of Lazarus is followed by a discussion of the Apocalypse.

As the initiation of the individual brings with it certain dangers, and the possibility of failure, and the price to be paid for it, so it is also with the initiation of mankind. This is the reason why John's Apocalypse abounds with images of terror and devastation. Human beings were not created to enjoy a comfortable existence in the material world and to forget their spiritual nature and their spiritual task. The Apocalypse is meant to remind us what this task is and of the consequences of failing in this task.

Although the process of mankind's initiation encompasses a span of time so vast that one can hardly imagine it, the distant future has to be prepared long before it becomes the present. We are in the situation of students whose final examinations are still a few years away but who have to pass interim exams all along the way. And the tests and trials of the path of the initiation of mankind have already begun – we live already in the Apocalypse. Mankind as a whole is already on the path – whether this is realised or not. Rudolf Steiner expressed this fact when he said that in our time mankind is 'crossing the threshold'.[2] Coming to the threshold, meeting the Guardian of the Threshold, are experiences on the path of initiation. And no matter how ignorant most people of our time are of what initiation is or means, they are swept along by the mighty current which takes mankind to the threshold of the spiritual world.

There are unmistakable signs that there is such a current. One of the symptoms of getting near to the threshold is a feeling of fear. And never before in the history of mankind have people so universally been dominated by a sense of anxiety and fear. Many of the problems of the present are engendered by fear. Even a major threat to our civilisation, the antagonism between world powers, is the result of mutual fear rather than any real aggressive intentions. And from the big clouds darkening our sky right down to inflation, recession, unemployment, drug-abuse, crime and all the private problems and worries, there is an endless array of things that people are afraid of. They do not realise that life has always been insecure here on earth and that in other ages people accepted disasters like famines, wars and plagues without living in constant dread of them. The truth is that the obsessive anxieties of our time are only the outward projections of an inner terror, the terror the soul feels when it stands at the abyss which separates the spiritual world from the world of the senses – the threshold. To be sure, there is much that could and should be changed in the relationship between person and person, nation and nation, mankind and nature – but no social or political or economic change would bring any benefit unless and until the fears that well up from the depth of the unconscious are overcome. And they can only be overcome by knowledge – spiritual knowledge.

No one would claim that having read a few books by Rudolf Steiner would allay all fears. One has to live with these thoughts until they become part of one's own being and then they show what they really are: a therapy for the anxiety neurosis of our time. This is also the reason why this knowledge was given: to counteract the mental epidemics which befall mankind in ever-increasing measure from now on. But these mental epidemics are the outward expression of the beginning of mankind's initiation, the crossing of the threshold.

At the threshold one meets the Guardian – but there are really two guardians. The Lesser Guardian is, one could say, a personal matter; he is concerned with the individual's approach to the threshold. But when it is a matter of mankind crossing the threshold, the Greater Guardian who is Christ stands there. This is the real meaning of this 'crossing' – to meet the Christ. And this is also the meaning of the etheric Christ-event of our time. This age which offers so little comfort to the soul in its physical aspect can find the great Comforter on the threshold. Initiation has at all times meant a freeing from the forces which bind humanity to the physical world. The conditions of the present and the fears they give rise to are the means to turn the minds of human beings from material concerns to the spirit and then to find the being who initiated Lazarus-John.

For Lazarus it was Christ in a physical body who performed the initiation. For mankind of the present it is the etheric Christ who is the Guardian of the initiation process in which we are all involved. This does not only mean the etheric vision of Christ, which is given to a few; it also means the experience of the Christ-impulse in the etheric world, which is the world of thought, of living thought. In this world every soul can find the Christ-impulse.

This is what Rudolf Steiner referred to when he said that it is Christ's language which we are meant to learn through spiritual science.[3] That language – no matter how abstract it seems – through which we learn about Saturn, Sun and Moon phases of evolution and the sequence of epochs on Earth, all these so-called 'anthroposophical teachings' are really a means of communication with the spiritual world, no less than any earthly tongue, and in the measure in which we learn with deep inwardness to speak this language, in that measure it will come to pass that Christ stands beside us and answers our questions.

The tests and trials of mankind's initiation have already begun and they will only become harder and more demanding in the future. But we have from the beginning the guidance of the great initiator of mankind, Christ. And this is also the first vision described in the book which speaks of mankind's initiation, the Apocalypse. John saw first 'One like unto the Son of Man.' This being is surrounded by seven candlesticks and he holds in his hand seven stars. These symbols refer to the mystery of time. On our clocks one hour is just like all the others. But this is not so with *real* time. Each hour is different in quality from the others and the same is true of days, years, centuries, millennia. And only a being who looks upon time from the heights of timeless eternity can know what is right in any given instant of time. It is he who guides the initiation of mankind to proceed at the right pace, in harmony with the course of time. And it is this real time which makes it necessary that the initiation of mankind has begun, that the Apocalypse has begun. It has become a commonplace to call the events of our time apocalyptic; one could only wish that the people who use the word would realise how appropriate it is.

16

The Four Riders of the Apocalypse

The Apocalypse of John is a subject Rudolf Steiner has treated on several occasions and the interpretation of the mysterious images of the book has been different every time. A truly esoteric work such as this is inexhaustible and no interpretation can be regarded as final. The Apocalypse can engender ever new insights in the souls ready to receive them.

In this chapter of *Christianity as Mystical Fact* the approach to the Apocalypse is dictated by the main theme: the ancient mysteries and Christianity. In this context the Apocalypse appears as a continuation of something which existed before the Christian era. In ancient Greece, for instance, the popular religion of the Olympic gods existed side by side with the deeper understanding that could be found in the mystery temples. In the same way – so it is stated in this chapter – since the Mystery of Golgotha, Christianity has existed as a religion open to all, as well as another more esoteric Christianity represented by the Apocalypse. It is a statement which is unlikely to find acceptance by any of the established churches. But even people less prejudiced may dislike the idea that there is one kind of Christianity for the common herd and another for a select group. However – and here lies the difference between the ancient mysteries and the new ones – it is not a human authority or even a divine one which makes the selection; it is the individual soul alone which decides whether to be satisfied with a simple faith or whether to seek a deeper understanding. In our time the capacity to live with a simple faith is disappearing and so there has to be an opportunity to find Christianity in its esoteric form.

The Apocalypse begins with John's vision of Christ who speaks to him: 'I am the Alpha and the Omega, the beginning and the end.' These words have to be understood as, 'In the "I am" is the Alpha and the Omega, the beginning and the end.' The Apocalypse is addressed to those who seek the Christ within the soul. For the exoteric Christian the Son of Man is a being outside and beyond him; on the esoteric path one seeks the Christ within.

Where does this seeking begin? The answer to this question is given in the interpretation of the first of the letters to the seven churches. This letter to the Church of Ephesus praises the members of that community for their Christian way of life but upbraids them for having forsaken the 'first love'. The interpretation given here is that the 'first love' is Christ and that it is not good enough to follow Christian principles in one's actions and behaviour; the Christ impulse must also be carried into one's thought life – not only in *what* one thinks but *how* one thinks.

Most people would say, 'Oh, if people would only act in accordance with Christian principles, then how they think and what they think would not matter at all.' But the Apocalypse is concerned with the esoteric inner path. Formal obedience to a set of moral precepts has no value on this path. It calls for a transformation of the soul-life and this transformation begins in the sphere of thought. The established churches have all, in this sense, forsaken the first love. They put spiritual truth in the form of dogma, so that it was removed from thought. And they want people to be good Christians in their actions, no matter what goes on in their thoughts.

This is not a point of view possible to the author of the *Philosophy of Freedom*, who regards any mere outward conformity with moral principles – with moral directives not found by one's own intuitions – as unfree and hence not truly moral.

It follows from this that thinking must be transformed in order to receive the right intuitions.

The transformation of thinking was, altogether, Rudolf Steiner's foremost concern. It is a theme that goes through his whole work, from the philosophic books to the Michael Letters. He never tired of telling the members of the need to strive in this direction. In a lecture given in 1923 he warned the anthroposophists not to follow the example of the theosophists who thought they had gone beyond materialism when they spoke of physical body, etheric body, astral body. But all they had in mind was that the physical body was dense matter, the etheric body a finer or thinner matter and the astral body a still finer substance. This kind of thinking is nothing but another kind of materialism, but less honest than the downright materialistic outlook. And finally Rudolf Steiner said:

> We have to take these things seriously. We ourselves
> have to examine whether we still cling to materialism
> and merely assign spiritual names to matter.
> A transformation of thinking and feeling is required
> if we wish to achieve a spiritual worldview.[1]

What, on this occasion, was simply called a new kind of thinking is really the entry of the Christ-impulse into the region of human thought and of human knowledge. And the letter to the Church of Ephesus in the Apocalypse can be understood as an exhortation to make the effort necessary for this transformation. The Apocalypse is itself a book which demands such a new kind of thinking. It is therefore not surprising that our ordinary untransformed thinking finds it incomprehensible. In this respect this last book of the Bible is indeed like the ancient mystery temples; it does not reveal its secrets to those who approach it with thoughts derived from the world of the senses.

The letters to the seven churches refer still to matters which lie within the scope of our normal waking consciousness.

The seven seals, however, take the reader to the higher level called 'Imagination' by Rudolf Steiner. The opening of these seals is introduced by a fundamental imagination: the highest Godhead surrounded by twenty-four elders and by the four beasts – Lion, Eagle, Bull and Human. The elders are beings who have advanced far beyond the present stage of mankind. They are, as it were, our elder brothers who have gone before us on the road we still have to travel. This image of the elders introduces therefore the main theme of the Apocalypse, the cosmic evolution of humanity and earth. It is in the course of this evolution that the beings above us have become what they are. And evolution is also the key to an understanding of the four beasts.

In the lectures *The Spiritual Hierarchies,* Rudolf Steiner speaks of the four stages of evolution, ancient Saturn, ancient Sun, ancient Moon and Earth. And then he reveals that each of these stages is under the rulership of a specific part of the zodiac. Saturn is ruled by the Lion, the Sun by the Eagle (the other name of the sign usually called Scorpio), the Moon by the Human Being (Aquarius the Waterman) and the Earth by the Bull. And seeing these beings – as John does in the Apocalypse – is a symbolic expression for beholding the course of world evolution, for 'reading the Akashic Record' as it is called.

But John is not only given a view of the past of the world. He sees in the hand of God a book sealed with seven seals, and only Jesus, the Lion of Judah, can open the seals. Judah, one of the twelve sons of Jacob, is indeed associated with the sign of the Lion and Jesus is his descendant. But there is a deeper reason why it is given to the Lion to open the seals. The power of the Lion was the ruler of the first stage of evolution, of ancient Saturn, the beginning of the world. Now, through the Mystery of Golgotha, there is again a new beginning here on Earth, the beginning of a future universe. Earth has become the 'Saturn-stage' of that future world and so once again the Lion forces come to the fore.

Ancient Saturn was a world which consisted only of warmth. The new beginning on Earth is also in the element of warmth – the warmth of the heart forces in human beings. This is the new Lion impulse which came with the Mystery of Golgotha. Christ is the bearer of this impulse. The whole future evolution of mankind and the world is bound up with this impulse and this is the reason why only the Lion of Judah can open the book in the hand of the Father-God, for this sealed book is the book of the future.

In one of the most difficult passages in his book Rudolf Steiner connects the four beasts with the four riders of the Apocalypse, a conception not found in any other book or lecture. But if it is understood that the nature of the Christ impulse is transformation, then it will also be clear that the fundamental powers of evolution – Lion, Eagle, Human, Bull – will themselves become transformed. They appear in mankind in a new form, and this is presented in the Apocalypse in the symbol of the four riders.

The first rider, with bow and arrow, represents war in the sense in which Heraclitus called war 'the father of all things'. Heraclitus also used the bow as a symbol for the polarities which are the foundation of all existence. The human heart – which corresponds to the sign Leo – holds the balance between the opposing currents of the arterial and venous blood. And the human being must find inwardly the Lion's courage to face the struggle between the Luciferic and the Ahrimanic forces. This is the connection between the first rider and the Lion.

The second rider, wielding a sword, is, paradoxically, concerned with peace. But he will not allow mankind earthly peace and contentment; his sword will take away this kind of peace, for it is the human being's destiny to strive, to labour and never to rest at any stage of development. What does it mean when we say, 'I am hungry?' It means that the stomach, the whole digestive system, demands *work*. It protests when there is no work for it. Earthly existence is only fruitful through work.

This urge to work is the human form of the power of Taurus the Bull, which is also the sign of fertility.

The third rider bears a pair of scales, the ancient symbol of justice. It is the principle which must rule the relationship between human beings. A true human relationship can only exist if we recognise and respect human dignity in each other. This sense for the equal rights of all people is the human form of the powers of the sign Aquarius the Waterman. What corresponds to this sign in human anatomy is the forearm. Unlike the forelimbs of animals, the lower arm has two bones which rotate in such a way as to make it possible that the hand can turn up or down. We can hold our hands up to receive something, or hold them in the reverse position when we are giving something. Giving and receiving, 'give and take', are the things which make human society function.

The fourth rider is 'death, and hell followed him'. What kind of ideal can one see in this gruesome picture? In one way or another in every human soul the desire exists to feel connected with something more permanent than one short earthly life. But there is nothing really permanent in the material world; even the stars above and the earth below us will pass away. And there is no better symbol of the transitory nature of the material world than our brain, which is continuously dying. It is almost a corpse even while we are alive. Yet this dying process makes it possible that we can think, that we can have ideas and ideals through which the spiritual world speaks to us, the world in which there is no death. And our thinking is the human form of the power, which is called Eagle when we consider the spiritual aspect, and Scorpion when we look upon the death process, without which we could only dream but not think. Through the Eagle we look up to what is beyond death – and this is religion.

If one reflects on the four riders of the Apocalypse and how they are interpreted in this chapter, it is not difficult to recognise in these descriptions the first faint outlines of the threefold social order as Rudolf Steiner gave it many years later.

17

The Fifth, Sixth
and Seventh Seals

We have to consider once again the great vision of John which
introduces the opening of the seals. He sees the Father God
in whose hand is the book sealed with seven seals and who
is surrounded by the twenty-four elders and by the four
beasts. Only the Lion of Judah can open the seals of the book.
But Jesus is also called the 'Lamb of God' in this part of the
Apocalypse. He is the Lion *and* the Lamb – in him war and
peace are one. This is again the concept of war as we have
found it in Heraclitus. It refers to the polarities which are at
the root of all existence: light and darkness, heaven and earth,
giving and receiving. But Christ is also the perfect equilibrium
between the polar opposites, and thus he brings peace between
the contending forces. He is both the Lion and the Lamb
and in this way fulfils the saying that with the coming of the
Messiah the Lion shall lie down with the Lamb.

And so the Lamb of God opens the seven seals one
after another. With the opening of the first four seals, one
after another, the four riders come. We already came to an
understanding that these riders represent the forces of the four
beasts in their human form. But after the four riders, three
further seals are opened by the Lamb. What can we expect from
the opening of these seals? Rudolf Steiner's interpretation is that
the cosmic impulses which have been reborn in mankind must
still be sanctified by the Christ-impulse. And what is revealed at

the opening of the last three seals are three phases in the Christening of the forces represented by the riders. And once again each of these phases is ruled by one of the four beasts.

At the time when John wrote the Apocalypse, humanity still lived in the epoch of the fourth rider, who represents, as we have seen, the human form of the Eagle forces. In fact John the Evangelist, who also wrote the Apocalypse, is himself traditionally associated with the Eagle symbol. And in the human being the Eagle-forces become the religious impulse, the inner need to look up to that which lies beyond death. The Eagle represents religion in the widest sense, but also in the narrow sense in which the word is commonly used. It was in this Eagle period that Christianity came into the world and so it could, at that time, only appear in the form of a religion beside other religions. Yet, as Rudolf Steiner expressed it, 'Christianity began as a religion but is greater than all religions.'[1]

The next phase, the opening of the fifth seal, must therefore bring a development of Christianity which takes it beyond the limits of a faith, a cult, or a church. This period of the opening of the fifth seal is our own time. And as the age of the fourth seal was ruled by the Eagle which soars to the heights, so our epoch is ruled by the earth-bound Bull. Nothing could demonstrate this change better than a comparison of the religious fervour of the Middle Ages with the purely material concerns of our time. There is a span of only about six hundred years between Richard the Lionheart, who led a Crusade, and James Watt, the Scotsman who developed the steam engine – yet they seem to have lived in different worlds. It is the difference between the impulses of the Eagle and the Bull.

However, the most characteristic feature of the forces of the Bull is the impulse to toil, to labour, to work. Under the rulership of these forces the human being is not allowed to exist in tranquillity or to feel contented. Although we have innumerable devices which are supposed to save work, there is less peace or tranquillity to be found now than there was in earlier times.

Yet the hustle and bustle of contemporary life is not the real aim of the Bull impulse. One could hardly imagine a better picture of peace and contentment than a grazing herd of cattle. Yet these animals are engaged in a most intense activity: in the process of digestion which, for them, is a spiritual activity. And in this intense spiritual activity they are at the same time at peace and in harmony with the cosmos. To carry spirit into matter is the true Taurus impulse.

When Christianity was under the Eagle influence, it had a tendency to reject the material world. Now – when the Lamb of God has opened the fifth seal – Christianity has to become a force that inspires human beings with love for the physical world and for work in it. If the Christian element in anthroposophy were only limited to speaking about the Mystery of Golgotha, it would be no more than an anachronistic continuation of the Eagle impulse. The true Christian nature of spiritual science manifests itself in its practical applications in medicine, education, agriculture, the arts. And even though in *The Agriculture Course* Rudolf Steiner does not mention the name of Christ, it is a profoundly Christian work in harmony with the cosmic forces of Taurus.

There is still another aspect of these forces to which attention must be paid. And once again the grazing cows illustrate this aspect. They are busy chewing and digesting their food. In the process of digestion a substance foreign to the body is taken in and assimilated; it becomes the body's own substance. When, at the time of the Eagle forces Christianity was a belief, a faith, it was not really assimilated, because it was not understood. In fact, right through the Middle Ages, it was generally accepted that human reason, human thinking, was incapable of understanding anything of a spiritual nature. Human reason could cope with the world of the senses but could not go beyond it. And what was given in the Bible was therefore to be accepted as divine revelation that one had to believe without question and without thinking.

And so Christianity – in spite of the religious fervour of that time – was not assimilated by the human soul. This too has to be radically changed in our age. No matter how hard it may seem, one has to 'chew' these difficult concepts again and again until they become truly one's own. Anthroposophical concepts are not, and must not, be easy to comprehend, for we live under the rule of Taurus, which demands toil. Unless we learn to ruminate spiritually as the cow ruminates physically, our beliefs could just as well be superstitions. We would not know the difference.

As the present epoch is ruled by the Bull, so the one that will follow it is under the rulership of Aquarius the Waterman. This influence was first revealed by the third horseman of the Apocalypse, who bears a pair of scales. It is the impulse to recognise the common humanity in every human being. This common humanity is of a divine nature, for what makes us truly human is only Christ's love for all mankind. And then Christianity will become a social force, of a power which the brutal selfishness of people in our time cannot even imagine.

At the opening of the last and seventh seal it is the Lion who becomes ruler of the epoch. And at that time the Lion-impulse will manifest itself in its most warlike form in the 'war of all against all'. Only a small group will then represent Christianity in its highest and most spiritual form. They are the seed of a new cycle that will come when that war has run its course of destruction.

With the vision of the four beasts and of the opening of the seals, John was given his first insight into the course of evolution. Such insights form an essential part of initiation. It was so in the ancient mystery temples and, as we can see from the Apocalypse, it is still so in the Christian mysteries. Why is there this necessity to know and to understand evolution – a process encompassing intervals of time too vast to be of any concern to us who live from day to day?

The grandiose images of evolution which unfolded before

the initiates were not experienced as we would experience a film show. The whole being of the initiates lived and took part in what they saw. And this kindled in them a fiery enthusiasm to work for this evolution, to become its devoted servants. The gods do not grant these visions in order to satisfy human curiosity, but in order to find among people on earth helpers filled with enthusiasm for their task.

Enthusiasm is altogether an essential element of evolution. In the Apocalypse it is said that the four beasts at the throne of God sing his praise, day and night unceasingly. This symbolic picture would be quite meaningless if it were taken literally. The only way in which God can be praised in a real sense is by enthusiasm for one's part in the great scheme of evolution. And this is what the Greek word *enthousiasmos* means – 'being in God'. The beings of the first hierarchy represented by the four beasts are 'enthusiasts' in this sense. The initiates of the ancient mysteries were, on the human scale, enthusiasts of this kind. But they kept their knowledge of evolution secret. It was not to be divulged to the shallow, trivial minds of the majority, who were incapable of such enthusiasm. Yet, in our time, the secrets of evolution *have* been made public and are open to all human beings. Why? Because every human soul must have the opportunity to find in itself at least some of that spiritual fire which is called enthusiasm.

In the context of all that has been said about the true nature of the Taurus impulse, with its emphasis on hard work, and in the context of the praising of God through enthusiasm, the following words of Rudolf Steiner are of special significance. The occasion for these remarks was that he had described some complicated spiritual facts and had, obviously, realised that his audience had not made the effort necessary to grasp what he had tried to convey. And so he said:

> You see it is really necessary that we should enter into these difficult details, otherwise we cannot arrive at an

exact understanding. I should very much welcome it if such knotty points were met not only by a certain passive acceptance, but – and this is so necessary for present-day man – that even for these difficult matters a little enthusiasm were aroused, a little keen participation.[2]

18

Inspiration and
Individual Responsibility

In the Apocalypse the opening of the seven seals is followed by the sounding of the seven trumpets. This is the symbolic expression of rising from the level of imagination to inspiration. It is necessary to come to a more concrete idea of what this means.

Imagination, the first stage of higher knowledge, is a transformation of thinking; inspiration can only be reached through a transformation of feeling. The first stage is, in comparison, easier because we are not as personally involved in our ideas as we are in regard to our emotions. If we were not so self-centred in our feelings, we would be open to inspirations from the spiritual world all the time. Yet the selfish streak in our feelings, which prevents us from receiving divine inspiration, is at the same time a protection because, being as we are and what we are, our souls could not stand the sounds of the heavenly trumpets. On the path to higher knowledge this protection has to be given up and this is a painful process.

We all shall get to know how painful this process is in life after death. The kamaloka period after death is the time when we are gradually purged of egotistic desires and wishes, hence the name purgatory. And only then can the soul ascend to the lower devachan, the spirit-land, which is the sphere of inspiration. An initiate such as John has to experience purgatory of his own free will while still incarnated in a physical body. This is the painful process which has to be endured in order to hear the voice of devachan, inspiration.

And now we can understand the interpretation Rudolf Steiner gives in this book of a significant scene described in the Apocalypse. An angel gives John a book and commands him to eat it. He obeys and the book is sweet as honey in his mouth but gives him pains in his stomach. Rudolf Steiner speaks of these two experiences in the reverse order. First comes the 'pain in the belly', which refers to the purgatory experience, and then follows the sweet taste in the mouth, which means the experience of the glory of lower devachan, the 'music of the spheres' as Pythagoras had called it, the world of inspiration.

But what John did out of his own free will, the purging of the soul while still incarnated in the physical world, is also a stage in the initiation of mankind as a whole. It is the destiny of every human soul to do what John has done when – after the great 'war of all against all' – the time of the sounding of the seven trumpets begins, which is only a few thousand years into the future. And for the souls who will not follow John's example, who will not impose on themselves the self-negations of purgatory – after all, it lies in our freedom – for these souls all the terrifying images of the Apocalypse will become harsh reality.

We can now ask what is meant by the 'book' which John has to swallow. It is the same book which is first mentioned in the Apocalypse as being in the hand of the Father-God. It is sealed with seven seals and only Christ, the Lamb of God, can open these seals. It is the book of evolution, the book in which the past and the future of mankind and the cosmos is set down. Before the God who exists in eternity, who is timeless, there is no past or future – for him they are one. As a person on a mountain peak looks down on the landscape before them, so God looks upon the events which, for us, pass in the course of time. This is the book sealed with seven seals. Only Christ, the Son of God, can open this book; but through Christ the book is opened to all human beings.

And the first person to whom it was given to read in this book was John and what he read he recorded in the Apocalypse.

However, it is not possible to read the book of evolution as one reads books here on earth. Only a soul which can direct its own evolution and so becomes an active participant in the evolutionary process can be allowed to know what the gods intend. John has become such a person who accepts full responsibility for his spiritual development. Evolution is no longer an *outside* current which carries him along; he himself becomes a part of this current. This is what is meant by the 'eating' of the book.

All human souls have gone through some development since the beginning of earth evolution, but this development was the work of higher beings. Just as the growing-up of a child is not his own doing but is done for him, so our spiritual development through many incarnations has been brought about by the spiritual hierarchies. And just as the natural growing-up comes to an end and any further maturing is up to the individual, so it is with mankind's spiritual evolution. From a certain point onwards it will be up to each individual. We must all at some point 'eat the book' and become individually responsible for our own further development.

Eating a book is perhaps a somewhat drastic picture but it is not so very far from the reality. There *is* a book which thousands of people have read and which leads straight into the reality at which the Apocalypse hints. It is Rudolf Steiner's *Knowledge of Higher Worlds*. The exercises suggested in this book, the forms of self-discipline described in it, are the beginning of becoming responsible for one's own evolution. But of the thousands of readers of this book only very few have 'eaten' it – meaning that they have practised what is suggested in it. And the sequel to the book, which Rudolf Steiner had intended, was never written because of this lack of response. But whatever the author had expected, in our time people do not feel any pressing need to take up exercises of this kind. It will not be like this in a not-so-distant future. Then these exercises will be necessary, if one wants to remain truly human – which means a being who is continually developing. Just as the animals have stayed behind humans in evolution, so the souls who will not 'eat the book' will stay behind the true human evolution.

The exercises given in the book are not the inventions of Rudolf Steiner. They have been known throughout the ages, but they were kept secret in the mystery schools. Only a small number of people were regarded as spiritually mature enough to become responsible for their own future evolution. But this selecting of people worthy of learning the secrets of spiritual development, necessary as it was, had a dark side. Those who followed the path of initiation in the mysteries could not help thinking of themselves as special individuals, as being better than the rest of mankind who had not found admittance to the mystery schools. And this meant that they were open to Lucifer's influence; they were vulnerable to Lucifer. This is the reason why the Nordic hero Siegfried was vulnerable on his back and why the Greek hero Achilles was vulnerable on his heel. In this way the myths expressed the fundamental weakness of the ancient mystery initiation. When Christ cursed the fig tree, the symbol of this initiation, he cursed the Luciferic element which was inseparable from it.

The initiation, the path of self-directed evolution, which the Apocalypse expresses in the image of John eating the book, is of a different nature; it is open to everyone, just as the book *Knowledge of Higher Worlds* can be read by everyone. No one is excluded. The individual soul itself chooses to be included or excluded. Yet, with the new initiation, with the eating of the book, a new mystery begins, more profound than anything hidden in the temples of antiquity. St Paul expressed it in the words, 'Not I, but the Christ within me.' The aim of the new initiation can only be to have the experience St Paul put into these simple words. And as there is only one Christ being, one might think that all individualities who come to this experience, who are transformed by this experience, become more or less the same and conform to a common pattern.

That is not so. The transformation makes the individual even more unique, even more his own being, and yet at the same time heightens the awareness of being part of a wholeness which is the brotherhood of humankind. This is the new mystery, the mystery of the Christ impulse: that it isolates the individuality and at the same time integrates it with all the other individualities that comprise mankind. On this path there is no danger of Luciferic pride or of Ahrimanic conformity. It is with this Christ mystery in view that Rudolf Steiner ends the chapter on the Apocalypse with the words:

> [T]he secrets of the ancient mysteries have been
> revealed through the events in Palestine. Through
> this has been unveiled what was before veiled in the
> mysteries. But there is now a new mystery; it is what
> the appearance of Christ has brought into the evolution
> of the world. The initiate of the ancient mysteries
> experienced in the spiritual world the direction of
> evolution towards the then still 'hidden Christ'.
> The Christian initiate experiences the hidden effects
> of the 'manifest Christ'.

What does Rudolf Steiner mean with this strange formulation 'the hidden effects of the manifest Christ'? The Christ-impulse comes to us in the form of our own individual intentions and aims. Within our own moral intuition, the Christ-impulse is hidden. These are the hidden effects of the Christ who became manifest in the Mystery of Golgotha. The initiation of the ancient mysteries was presented to the world in the symbolic images of mythology. We have already seen that the myths of Heracles, Odysseus and Theseus are descriptions of initiation experiences. It became necessary to give mankind a Christian equivalent of such myths. It is the legend of Parsifal and the Holy Grail.

Parsifal leaves the forest in which he was brought up, with the intention of becoming one of the knights of King Arthur.

But Arthur and the Knights of the Round Table – although the saga treats them as Christians – are really following a pre-Christian tradition. They are a hand-picked elite and, as they have to be of noble blood, they depend on group-soul forces. The whole principle of nobility, of a class superior by ancestry, is based on faith in the forces of the group-soul. Although Parsifal is himself of noble descent, he is not meant to become a knight of this kind. He is prevented from joining King Arthur's court and then, having come to Montsalvat, the Castle of the Grail, fails to ask the right question.

This failure makes him almost an outcast; he wanders through the world lonely, isolated. Filled with bitterness about his fate he even rejects the comfort of religion; he enters no church and offers no prayer to God. Yet, after years of this kind of life, he is once again admitted to the Castle of the Grail, asks the right question and becomes the new Grail King. What is it that opened the doors of Montsalvat to Parsifal? It is not his noble ancestry, it is no deed of knightly valour, but these years of loneliness, of separation even from God, have made him an individuality, a soul that can give itself direction, a soul that can become responsible for its own future evolution. The elite corps of Arthur and his knights was inevitably open to the forces of Lucifer and was ultimately destroyed by them. The path to the Grail is for individuals. This is what Rudolf Steiner meant by 'the hidden effects of the manifest Christ'.

19

The Time of Jesus

The next chapter of *Christianity as Mystical Fact,* about the historical background of the life of Jesus, deals mainly with the brotherhood of the Essenes. This too is a subject which Rudolf Steiner has treated differently on different occasions. In the present context, the Essenes have to be seen as an intermediary stage between spiritual truth for a few, in the ancient mysteries, and spiritual truth for all mankind, in the new mysteries of Christianity. The Essenes cultivated spiritual knowledge and spiritual development within a community. They too followed a path of initiation which was kept secret and not divulged to the outside world.

The Essenes lived in small communities where the members had to subject themselves to strict regulations and to a very frugal lifestyle. They were celibate, the consumption of meat and alcohol was forbidden and there was only one meal a day, which consisted of bread, salt and water. The main occupation was the study of holy books, meditation and prayer. As the paramount aim of this life was spiritual development, initiation, the members of the community should not be diverted from this aim by any outside interests or concerns. They existed, therefore, in a kind of isolation from the ordinary people.

In his lectures on the Gospel of Matthew, Rudolf Steiner gives some indication of the Essene initiation knowledge.[1] At the centre of this knowledge was the Tree of the Sephirot, an arrangement of ten concepts or principles which were regarded as forming the fundamental spiritual structure of the world.

These ten principles, the Sephirot, and their interrelations, in later centuries became the basis of a Jewish school of esotericism, the kabbalists.

When an Essene had contemplated the Tree of the Sephirot for a longer or shorter period, when he had immersed his whole being in these ten principles, a time came when he no longer felt himself as a separate entity but as a living part of the cosmos, just as a branch is a living part of a tree. He had become a 'branch' which in Hebrew is *netzer*. Such a *netzer* founded an Essene community in a locality which was called 'the place of *netzer*', or Nazareth. In the course of time other people who were not Essenes settled in the vicinity of this community. Among them were the parents of Jesus. So it came that Jesus grew up in Nazareth and knew the Essenes from his early childhood, but he never joined their brotherhood and their way of life. In Rudolf Steiner's lectures *The Fifth Gospel*, one can find the reasons why he disagreed with the principles of the Essene order. Their spiritual development was only possible under the special conditions in which they lived and which amounted to a withdrawal from ordinary life, the life of the rest of mankind. Jesus condemned such a withdrawal.

The ascetic lifestyle of the Essenes was really foreign to the Jewish religion. Although the Essenes were Jews, they combined the Jewish tradition with a very different spiritual impulse, namely that which came from Buddha. The Buddhists were the first who formed monastic communities of the kind which later appeared within the Jewish tradition in the form of the Essene brotherhood.

But there is an even deeper connection between the Essenes and Buddha. There are beings of a higher nature than humans, yet who incarnate in human form in order to guide and to help mankind's evolution: they are called Bodhisattvas. These beings, too, go through a development. When a Bodhisattva reaches the next higher stage he becomes a Buddha, and once he has become a Buddha he no longer incarnates on earth. When this happens another Bodhisattva begins his ascent to Buddhahood, an ascent which goes through many incarnations. This happened also when the Gautama Buddha had finished his last life on earth. Another Bodhisattva began his earthly pilgrimage. And this Bodhisattva who will become a Buddha – the Maitreya Buddha of the future – was, in one of his incarnations, about a century before Christ, a greatly revered teacher in the order of the Essenes. His name was Jeshu ben Pandira. He came into conflict with the Orthodox Jewish priesthood and was stoned to death. So, through this 'teacher of righteousness', as he is called in the Dead Sea Scrolls, the Essenes were related to the spiritual stream represented by the Gautama Buddha.

Although with the Mystery of Golgotha the sectarian spirituality of the Essenes was no longer justified, it must not be forgotten that before the Christ event, the order represented a step away from the radical exclusivity of the mystery temples and a step nearer to the Christian ideal. It is therefore not surprising that a higher being, a Bodhisattva, connected himself with this movement at one time. In fact, a being of this kind must have found the Essenes the best of three possible choices open to him in Palestine. In the century before the Mystery of Golgotha three religious groups existed among the Jews. They are of historical interest, simply as the background to the events recounted in the New Testament, but as we shall see later, they are still relevant to us today.

These three groups were the Pharisees, the Sadducees and the Essenes. The Pharisees held fast to the original teaching of Moses. For them every word in the Old Testament, every law and rule laid down at the time of the great prophet, was considered valid for all times, unchanged and unchangeable. Because of this strict adherence to the Mosaic tradition, they were implacably hostile to the Roman conquerors. It was the Pharisees who, thirty years after the crucifixion, instigated a rebellion against the Romans, which ended with the destruction of Jerusalem in AD 70 and the expulsion of the Jews from their ancient homeland.

Any Jew could, if he so wished, join the Pharisees, but not every Jew could become a Sadducee. One had to be born as a

member of a certain family, a very large family, which had for
many generations monopolised the rank of the High Priest
in the Temple of Jerusalem. Caiaphas, the High Priest whose
intrigues led to the crucifixion of Jesus, was a Sadducee. And a
hundred years earlier it was also the Sadducees who had Jeshu
ben Pandira, the Bodhisattva who was a leading Essene, stoned
to death. The Sadducees, in spite of their high standing in the
ministry of the Jewish religion, were, one could say, extremely
flexible compared with the Pharisees. For them truth was
not something contained in the books of Moses; truth was
whatever happened to be convenient or advantageous. And so
the Sadducees got on very well with the Romans.

The third group, the Essenes, had neither the rigid
dogmatism of the Pharisees nor the ruthless opportunism of
the Sadducees. They had left behind all worldly considerations
and were only concerned with their spiritual development. It
was a genuine striving for the reality of spiritual experiences –
neither a hanging on to a tradition (the Pharisee attitude) nor
a cynical indifference to the spirit (the Sadducee attitude). And
if Jeshu ben Pandira, the Bodhisattva, had to find disciples he
could only find them among the Essenes.

These three groups also show what would have been the fate
of all mankind if the Mystery of Golgotha had not taken place.
Eventually all human souls would have been either clinging to
some tradition, or cheerfully ignoring such religious traditions,
or seeking salvation on a spiritual path which is incompatible
with the conditions of ordinary life. This development would
have been inevitable, because in every one of us there lurks a
Pharisee, a Sadducee and an Essene.

Rudolf Steiner spoke of these three temptations in every
soul in a lecture given in the Esoteric School.[2] The Pharisee
in us wants any truth he has learned to be absolute, the last
word on the subject, to which nothing could be added. The
Sadducee is inclined to believe that any view which brings him
personal advantage, or simply comforts him in being as he is,
must automatically also be the truth. And the Essene seeks

some inner illumination while losing touch with the wisdom and the truth which is all around us in the world. As Rudolf Steiner pointed out in the lecture, it is not a matter of trying to get rid of these three temptations but of making them balance each other. It is the right balance between the Pharisee, the Sadducee and the Essene in us which is necessary for spiritual progress. But, of course, it is necessary to recognise when the dogmatist, the opportunist or the mystic try to counsel us.

There is still another aspect of these three groups to consider. The Pharisee looks back to the past; he wants to preserve a truth that was valid at some time, for all times. The Sadducee lives in the present; he will change his views if, under present conditions, this would be to his advantage. But in the other-worldliness of the Essene there is something reaching into the present which will be in its right place in the future.

This is the reason why Rudolf Steiner spoke on other occasions of anthroposophy as preparing for a new form of Essene life.[3] When we remember the teaching of the Apocalypse that in future humanity must learn to overcome all hankering after material satisfaction – when we consider that the sixth post-Atlantean epoch is the age of human brotherhood – then we can see in faint outline a community life of the future, less concerned with material comforts than the present civilisation, but imbued with a far greater sense of 'togetherness.' This will not be a civilisation of big cities. In fact, the flight from the city has already begun and what will develop in the future are small village communities. Rudolf Steiner mentioned in this context the old Russian village community called *mir* as a forerunner of this future form.[4] If one takes all these indications together, then the Essene communities appear in a different light. If one looks at them as the first – and necessarily crude – form of something that will only be perfected in the future, one can understand why Jeshu ben Pandira, the Buddha of the future, taught among them. And one can also understand why Rudolf Steiner in this chapter about the background of the life of Jesus draws special attention to them.

20

The Spirit in Christianity

The next chapter of *Christianity as Mystical Fact* bears the title 'The Essence [or Nature] of Christianity'. One cannot expect that such a subject would be dealt with in a simple fashion, nor is it easy for the modern mind to comprehend the religious controversies of the early centuries of Christianity. Yet behind the acrimonious debates of that period there lies a fundamental issue which has not been resolved to this day and which concerns the very core of Christianity. In the previous chapters of the book we have been shown that the Mystery of Golgotha came as a fulfilment of the ancient mysteries. Yet – and this is emphasised in this chapter – there was almost from the beginning of Christianity disagreement with the wisdom of the mysteries on a crucial question.

The mystery-teaching spoke of the eternal in the human being, the immortal or divine, which is different from the earthly and mortal personality. The eternal part goes from incarnation to incarnation, assuming every time a different personality. For the mysteries this eternal was all-important, while the transient, earthly personality was of little account. The immortal part of man was the 'Logos' – in every human soul there was something of this Logos, in some more, in others less; but in order to find the Logos, to experience it, the earthly personality had to be left behind.

And now came the Christians and said, 'the being you call Logos became a man and united itself with a particular personality, Jesus of Nazareth, and anyone who worships Jesus also finds in him the Logos.' The Christians looked up to an earthly personality, Jesus, in whom was also the Logos or, as they called him, Christ. And unlike the mysteries, the Christians therefore valued the earthly personality.

So there was a fundamental difference between the mystery tradition and Christianity, a clash between two sets of values: one which regarded the earthly personality as a prison from which mankind must strive to free itself, and one which felt that the earthly personality was saved and redeemed by Jesus Christ. If one were to translate this conflict into more familiar terms one could say that the mysteries had more regard for the human spirit, the Christians more for the soul. And the difficulty for the modern mind consists in this – that both terms, spirit and soul, have lost any concrete meaning.

It was a council of bishops which in AD 869 in Constantinople took the Christian position to its extreme and decided that it was heresy to believe that the human being had a spirit; human beings had a soul with some spiritual attributes. The European mind has been dominated by this dogma for more than a thousand years and so has no idea about what is meant by 'spirit'. And then came modern science and did away with the concept of a human soul. It was said that the human body is a complicated mechanism but, all in all, simply a machine – and to speak of a soul in it was like assuming a ghost to be present in a machine. And so the modern mind, having been robbed of any understanding of the nature of spirit or soul, stands baffled before the controversies of the early Christian centuries.

But what may seem to us a quite meaningless argument affected people in those days very deeply. An outstanding example is the Emperor Julian. He is called the Apostate in the history books because, at a time when Christianity had already been accepted in Rome (and he had been brought up in it), he renounced the Christian faith, reintroduced the worship of the pagan gods and was initiated in the Eleusinian mysteries. The rumours that he was murdered by a Christian illustrate how deeply people felt about these questions at that time.

However, in order to understand the conflict, one has to go beyond events in the physical world. When the pre-Christian mysteries were still at their height, when they still provided a link between mankind and the spiritual world, the initiates of these mysteries who had freed themselves from the earthly personality, which means from the earthly self, found in the spiritual world a mighty being who bestowed on them a higher self, a spirit-self. The initiates knew this being as the Sun Spirit. But in the course of time it became less and less possible to have this experience. And if nothing else had happened, the mysteries would have ceased to be a link with the spiritual world and there would have been nothing to take their place. People on earth would then only know themselves as earthly personalities; they would forget their spiritual nature altogether. This is the reason why the Sun Spirit descended and united himself with Jesus of Nazareth. He united himself with an earthly personality so that human beings, as earthly personalities, could reach him and through him awaken the eternal in themselves.

The initiate of the ancient mysteries had to forsake his earthly personality and only then, as a pure spirit, could he meet the Logos, the Sun Spirit. Through the Mystery of Golgotha, earthly personalities can find in Jesus Christ the Sun Spirit here on earth and, through him, awaken the pure spirit hidden in their souls. Rudolf Steiner has expressed this Christian mystery in the Christmas verse of the *Soul Calendar* which, in a free translation, reads:

> I feel, as if awakened from enchantment,
> The spirit-child within the womb of the soul.
> The holy cosmic Word (Logos) has engendered
> In the heart's day-bright consciousness
> The hopeful fruit of heaven which now in jubilation
> Expands into the world from
> The divine foundations of my soul.

Not outside the soul, the personality, but *within* the soul, the spirit-child begotten by the Logos, is born. But what these words describe is not something which happens naturally; it is the result of a path of initiation, the new Christian initiation. The early Christians who decreed that the human being has no spirit also rejected the idea of initiation. It was not necessary. Belief in Christ was enough to ensure immortality. And the people who adhered to ancient traditions of initiation rejected the idea that the transitory earthly personality could find within itself the immortal spirit. Both sides misunderstood the nature of the Mystery of Golgotha.

The incarnation of Christ in Jesus took place so that all people could become initiates even when they were still earthly personalities. This is the real purpose of Christianity or, as Rudolf Steiner expressed it in the title of his chapter, the essence of Christianity. It was due to the unceasing efforts of the Church of Rome that this essence of Christianity remained unknown to the vast majority of Christians. For centuries anything appertaining to initiation was suppressed, destroyed, persecuted. But there were, from the beginning, Christians who were aware of the real mission of Christianity. One of them was St Paul. Paul was, before his conversion, a Pharisee. The Pharisees, narrow-minded traditionalists as they were, also had traditions of esoteric knowledge, of mystery wisdom. And when Paul had the Christ-experience on the road to Damascus he also gained an understanding of the new mysteries.

We have seen before that there was a conflict between the tradition which valued the eternal spirit in the human being and the Christians who valued the earthly personality. In Paul this outer conflict became a conflict within himself. He was at all times aware of his faults and weaknesses, of his unworthiness as a person, and yet he could say in deep humility, 'Not I, but the Christ within me.' This too is part of the essence of Christianity, part of the new initiation, the awareness of the light of the spirit and the darkness of the soul in oneself. In this way what was once a religious conflict on the plane of history still exists as an inner struggle.

Paul had, as was mentioned, esoteric knowledge, mystery knowledge, through his connection with the Pharisees. This was not a knowledge he could share with everybody. He could speak about his Christ-experience to all, but, among the people he converted to Christianity on his travels, there were some to whom he could also impart his mystery knowledge, which was now illuminated by the Christ-experience. One such man he found in Athens – Dionysius the Areopagite. Through Dionysius the esoteric teaching of Paul was passed on for many generations, but only by word of mouth. It was only five centuries later that this teaching was written down and attributed to the Areopagite. Modern scholars do not accept the writings to be by Dionysius the Areopagite, calling the author Pseudo-Dionysius. However, Rudolf Steiner spoke of the tradition that each leader of the esoteric school founded by Dionysius the Areopagite was given the name Dionysius. And in this chapter of *Christianity as Mystical Fact,* he mentions the writings of Dionysius. Moreover, in Steiner's own books and lectures he used the names of the hierarchies as they are given in the writings of Dionysius: Angels, Archangels, Archai, Exousiai, Dynameis, Kyriotetes, Thrones, Cherubim, Seraphim.

Dionysius the Areopagite does not only speak of the hierarchies but goes above them to the Holy Trinity. And it is here, when he approaches the mystery of the Father God, that for the modern reader he becomes incomprehensible. What he says is that the Father God neither exists nor does he not exist. He is above the world in which something either exists or does not exist. Rudolf Steiner's commentary to this mystifying statement points out that our concepts of existence and non-existence are derived from the sense-world and are thus not applicable to the highest divinity. The Father God has to be thought of as 'above being'. If one follows the line of thought indicated by this comment, one realises that we use the concept 'existence' only in connection with something specific.

It is a definite thing or creature or being which we regard as existing or whose existence we deny. Even when we speak of spiritual beings, angels or cherubim, we have to think of their existence as being of a particular kind. The Father God is not anything particular or specific – that is why all the infinity of beings to whom he gave existence can find in him their 'home'.

In the Oberufer *Shepherds' Play* the Star-Singer thanks God for the stars and then for 'the darkness which makes them so bright'. In the peasant wisdom of this ancient Christmas play there is the perfect image for the obscure teaching of Dionysius the Areopagite. Without the darkness we could not see the stars at all. We are quite certain that the stars exist. But does the darkness exist in the same way as the stars exist? The darkness neither is – nor is not.

In the first centuries after the Mystery of Golgotha there were various groups of Christians who tried to reconcile mystery wisdom with Christianity, as did Dionysius. Some of these groups called the Father God 'he who is not'. They meant the same thing as Dionysius. The general name for these groups is Gnostics. We shall discuss them next. But it will be clear from the example of Gnostic thinking – the God who is and is not – why the ancient mysteries withheld their concepts from the multitude and why St Paul did not tell all his converts what he told Dionysius the Areopagite of Athens.

21

The Gnostics

In the fourth century BC the Archangel Michael was the regent of the age, just as he is again in the present age. The Michael impulse is cosmopolitan; it wants to break down national and racial barriers, and if human beings on earth do not freely and voluntarily follow this impulse it will find other means to force things in the right direction. Much of the social and political upheavals of our time are such forceful manifestations of the Michael impulse. In the fourth century BC it was also necessary to change human attitudes by force, but at that time a single personality was used as the instrument to bring about this change. This was Alexander the Great. With a relatively small army he conquered Greece, Asia Minor, Egypt and Persia, and even entered India. This vast empire broke up immediately after his death, but the real purpose of the conquests was not political; it was spiritual. And this purpose, to bring about a meeting and mingling of different cultures, was achieved. For the first time in history a truly cosmopolitan culture arose.

When, a few centuries later, Christianity spread from its origin in the Holy Land to all parts of Europe, it could not have done so if there had not been the preparation of a culture which was international. The centre of this culture was a city founded by Alexander himself, Alexandria, at the mouth of the Nile. It was here that the astronomical wisdom of Babylon, the medical knowledge of Egypt and the Sun worship of Persia all came together and were illuminated by the clarity of Greek thought.

The ancient mystery centres had been designed for the needs of particular nationalities, now the different mystery streams came together in preparation for the new mystery that was for all mankind, the Mystery of Golgotha.

It was the Christianity of the Gnostics which drew wisdom from the ancient mysteries in order to understand the Christ event. *Gnosis* is Greek for 'knowledge' and, unlike the Church of Rome which wanted the human mind limited to faith, the Gnostics sought to bring the light of understanding into their faith. However, it has to be said that what little Gnostic writing escaped destruction by Roman Christianity is for us of an almost impenetrable obscurity. In the first of the so-called Grail lectures Rudolf Steiner drew attention to our difficulty in understanding Gnostic texts.[1]

He mentioned in this context that what took place in the first centuries after the Mystery of Golgotha was a change in human thought. It reached a depth such as had never existed before or after. It was a time when men of true religious and philosophic genius lived. Rudolf Steiner went on to give an example of this profound Gnostic thought. Although he did not mention the name, the ideas presented are those of the great Gnostic teacher Valentinus. According to this view, before there was anything at all there was the Father who is also called Bythos, which means the 'abyss' or the 'profundity', and there was Sige, which means 'silence.' Creation began when Bythos mated with Sige and she brought forth Anthropos (the cosmic human being) and Aletheia (truth).

They engender further beings who in turn produce offspring until there are altogether thirty spiritual beings. They are called Aeons, and they are not just 'beings': every Aeon is a whole world. And each successive world is a stage lower than the one before. Our own world, the world we experience through our senses, is the thirty-first and the lowest of all these worlds. This world of ours is the work of a being far less exalted than the Aeons. It is called the Demiurgus, which approximately means the 'cosmic artisan'. And that this, our world, is far from perfect, is due to the limited abilities of its maker, the Demiurgus. In fact Valentinus, like many other Gnostics, identified this Demiurgus with Yahweh, the God of the Old Testament. Unlike the Jews and the Christians who accepted the Old Testament, the Gnostics had no reverence for Yahweh. But they also did not make the mistake of believing that the God of the Old Testament was the Father – the God who is 'above being and not-being,' the Abyss.

In the next higher world above ours – the thirtieth world in successive descent from the Father – is the Aeon called Sophia, 'wisdom'. This wisdom-being was once filled with a great longing to see the radiant light of the Father, which, from so far down in the sequence of worlds, was not visible. But this wish of Sophia could only be fulfilled on one condition: she had to free herself of something that was part of her own being. She had to expel this part from her nature. And what she had to expel – and did – was desire. Desire became a separate being called Achamod (meaning not known) which was banished from the world of Sophia and entered our world. This is why our world, and we ourselves, are filled with desire. But there lives in Achamod a deep longing to be reunited with Sophia.

And once for one cosmic moment a divine light fell upon Achamod. That light-moment has never been forgotten, and that is why there is in human souls a longing for Sophia, wisdom, and a seeking for the divine light. This divine light that once shone upon Achamod did not come from any Aeon, it did not come from the Father; it came from God the Son, the Logos. There are really two lines of descent from the Father. In one line are the generations of Aeons described before; in the other line of descent are God the Son, or Logos, and God the Holy Spirit. And when the Logos became a man at the Mystery of Golgotha these two lines of descent from the Father came together and became one.

This is – in bare outline – the content of what the Gnostic Valentinus called the Gospel of Truth. It seems like a kind of mythology but is far more confusing than any myth.

Rudolf Steiner told this strange myth, in greater detail than is given here, to his audience. Since he had earlier on praised the profound thoughts of the Gnostics, the people present at this lecture (and many readers ever since) must have felt quite at a loss what to make of this story. Yet Rudolf Steiner offered no help, nor did he provide any interpretation then or later. What he said at the end of the lecture was more or less to the effect that if his listeners felt mystified, that was just what he wanted them to feel. So it is up to the reader to interpret this Gnostic myth as was done with other myths in this book.

The Father God who is above being and not-being is in himself unknowable. This is already implied in the words of Christ, 'No one comes to the Father except through me' (John 14:6). The hidden Father reveals himself through Christ, the Logos, the Word. We are so familiar with the first sentence of the Gospel of John – 'In the beginning was the Word' – that we feel no sense of wonder at this statement. The Gnostic thinkers *did* have a sense of wonder and they understood that the Word could only be spoken into Silence. The cosmic Word resounded and there was Silence to receive it. But what was meant by this Silence was not merely absence of sound. The Gnostics were familiar with spiritual practices and knew from experience an inner silence, an inner stillness, which is not only a muting of feelings and thoughts, an absence of inner clamour, but a *presence*.

The disciples of Valentinus in particular had to come to the experience of this Silence, and since it was thought that outer silence was conducive to the inner reality, Valentinus imposed a condition of five years' silence on anyone aspiring to become his pupil. Some of this ancient tradition has survived in the Trappist monks' vow of silence and in the silent prayers of the Quakers. But for the Gnostics the reality which they met in the inner silence of their souls was a minute reflection of the immensity of the Silence into which the Word of God was spoken.

From the Father and Silence there descended not only the Logos, the Word, but also Anthropos, the human being, and Aletheia, truth. This being Anthropos is what Rudolf Steiner called 'the religion of the gods'.[2] He said that just as we human beings have religions in which we pay homage to gods, so the gods have *their* religion and what they look up to is the cosmic human being: that is, the Father-God's Idea of the Human Being. Our ideas are shadows without reality, but the ideas of the Creator-God are real entities, spiritual beings. And Anthropos, the Father's Idea of the Human Being, is such an exalted spirit that it is the religion of the gods. We know this Anthropos of the Gnostics under another name: Adam Kadmon, the heavenly Adam.

The Aeons are in pairs, and as the Aeon Father is accompanied by the Aeon Silence, so the Aeon Anthropos is accompanied by Aletheia. It is one of the most profound insights of the Gnostic world-conception that the concept of Human Being is inseparable from the concept Truth. The Wisdom of the Father-God could create beings and worlds without end, and yet this wisdom would not be known unless there was a being who could recognise it as wisdom. This being is the Human Being and its ability to recognise wisdom is what the Gnostics called Aletheia. Humankind has been, from the beginning of the world, the bearer of truth – one could say God's organ for Truth, as the human eye is an organ for light. When earthly humanity had lost this Truth, Christ came to restore it to them and this is implied in the words 'I am the Way, the Truth and the Life' (John 14:6).

However, the disposition for truth is embedded very deeply in the human organisation, right down in the physical body which came into being already on ancient Saturn. And that is why we can recognise truth long before our conscious reasoning has grasped it. Rudolf Steiner counted on this inborn sense of truth when he spoke of spiritual connections which are, to begin with, beyond our understanding. Of course, there is still the obligation to make the necessary effort to come to a conscious understanding, but at first there is a moment of unconscious intuition: 'This is true.'

The Gnostics too valued this instinctive sense of truth and called it *Pistis,* faith. For them faith did not mean believing what one cannot know and cannot understand, it meant *recognising* truth as a first step towards understanding it.

These first four Aeons, the Father, Silence, Anthropos, Truth, exist as it were before the beginning of time – that means before the Saturn stage of evolution. The Aeons which follow the first four in descending order are divided into three groups. There is a group of four Aeons which – in our terminology – corresponds to Ancient Saturn, a group of twelve which corresponds to the Ancient Sun, and a group of ten corresponding to the Ancient Moon. And among these Moon-Aeons we find Sophia, wisdom.

What the Gnosis of Valentinus recounts of Sophia – her longing for the light of the Father and that she cast out desire in order to see the light – refers to events on the ancient Moon described in Rudolf Steiner's *Outline of Esoteric Science.* In the course of the Moon-evolution mankind received the astral body; it contained, like the astral body of present-day animals, instinctive wisdom and instinctive desires. At this stage Sun and Moon were still one cosmic body. But then the Sun left the Moon and with the Sun went all the finer substances and forces, leaving the cruder forces behind. This division also affected the astral body. The finer part went with the Sun; this is the spirit-self or manas – or the Sophia of the Gnostics. The crude astral forces remaining on the Moon are to a large extent still in us – this is Achamod. But there is also in us Achamod's longing to be reunited with Sophia. We call it 'desire for knowledge'.

And what was the divine light that once fell upon Achamod? In the same course of lectures in which Rudolf Steiner spoke of the Gnosis of Valentinus he described certain deeds Christ had performed for mankind long before the Mystery of Golgotha. After the Fall of Man in ancient Lemuria, the human astral body became helpless against the sense impressions; anything humans experienced through their senses either aroused an irresistible desire or an equally powerful revulsion. The soul was continuously torn between these uncontrollable urges. And then Adam Kadmon – the Anthropos of the Gnostics – in the spiritual world turned to Christ for help for mankind. And Christ united himself with the Adam Kadmon being, who is the archetype of humankind. Through Adam Kadmon flowed the healing forces of Christ into the human organisation on earth. And the twelve senses became the neutral, balanced organs of perception that they are now. But this deed of Christ was the occasion when Achamod – desire – experienced the light of the Logos.

One can see from this example of a Gnostic tradition the profound knowledge that once existed in connection with Christianity. It was different from the Gnosis of our time, from anthroposophy, because that ancient knowledge could still speak to imaginations, to imaginative powers of the human soul which we have lost. The Gnostics would not have needed (and would not have understood) our explanation or interpretation of the Gnosis of Valentinus. Yet there is a spiritual kinship between our striving and the path of the Gnostics. And this kinship is implied in the very name of our movement: Anthropos is the first of the Aeons born of the Father and Silence; Sophia is the last of the thirty Aeons; together they are Anthropo-Sophia – mankind's knowledge of itself.

22

The *Pistis Sophia* and the *Acts of John*

The lecture in which Rudolf Steiner outlined the teaching of the Gnostic Valentinus was given on December 28, one of the twelve holy nights. Christmas was altogether a time when he often referred to Gnostic traditions. After all, even the idea of Sophia belongs to that tradition. And the 'forgotten faith' of the Gnostics offers indeed a purer vision of the Christ-event than is expressed in the sentimental and commercialised Christmas celebrations of our time.

Only fragments of this Gnostic Christianity exist, and only because they escaped, by chance, destruction by the adherents of the Church who denied even the possibility of knowledge, Gnosis, of the spiritual world. The largest and most important of these fragments is a manuscript dating from the second century known as *Pistis Sophia* (faith and wisdom). The main part of this Gnostic text is taken up by Christ describing to the disciples his descent from the highest spheres through the Aeons down to earth. However, there is also much else in this work. In a lecture given during another holy night, Rudolf Steiner spoke of a prayer contained in the *Pistis Sophia* and he said:

[It] is not just an invented prayer but that is what Christ, after he had passed through the Mystery of Golgotha, taught those to pray who could still understand him in the time which he spent with his more close disciples after overcoming the Mystery of Golgotha.

And that is part of the understanding, the Gnostic knowledge which these disciples were still able to bring to Christ at that time and which has disappeared in the way I indicated about the time, about the centuries when the Mystery of Golgotha happened.[1]

In these words Rudolf Steiner confirms what the *Pistis Sophia* claims in its first sentence: that it is the teaching Christ gave to the disciples after the resurrection. That this teaching needs a special kind of understanding – which existed then but does not exist now – will become clear from the text of the prayer and Rudolf Steiner's interpretation of it. The words of the prayer are:

> I want to glorify you, O Light, because I want to
>   come to you.
> I want to glorify you, O Light, because you are my
>   Saviour.
> Do not leave me in chaos,
> Save me O Light in the heights, because it is you
>   whom I have glorified.
> You sent me your light through you and saved me.
> You have led me to the higher place of chaos.
> May the spawn of evil which pursue me sink down in
>   the lower places of chaos.
> And do not let them come to the higher places so that
>   they see me.
> And may great darkness cover them and darkness on
>   top of that.
> And do not let them see me in the light of your
>   strength which you have sent me to save me so
>   that they do not gain power over me again.
> And the counsel they have taken to take from my
>   strength from me, let it not succeed,
> And how they have said words against me to take my
>   light from me.

Rather take theirs from them instead of mine.
And they said they would take all my light and they
were not able to take it because the strength of
your light was with me.
Because they took counsel without your
commandment, O Light, that is why they were not
able to take my light.
Because I have believed in the Light, I will not be
afraid.
And the Light is my Saviour. And I will not be afraid.[2]

One can find this prayer beautiful, but without the explanation given by Rudolf Steiner, one cannot understand what is prayed for in these words. In the lecture where this prayer is quoted, Rudolf Steiner explains first how our memory pictures come about. Our etheric body contains various kinds of etheric forces, among them the forces of the light-ether. When we meet a person for the first time this inner light-ether vibrates in a certain way and these vibrations strike the physical body. When we meet the same person later on for the second time, the light-ether responds with the same vibration, which strikes the physical body, and we recognise that this is Mr X whose acquaintance we have made some time ago. Of course, we have to be awake for such a recognition and, when we are awake, part of the I and the astral body is in the light-ether of the world outside. We could not see anything at all if the I and the astral body were not in the light-ether around us. And in the act of recognition the human soul (I and astral body) look from the outer light-ether upon the inner light-ether. Our whole memory is like this: a beholding of the inner light from the outer light.

That we are not aware of this, that we are only aware of the memory pictures which arise, is due to Ahriman. Ahriman has bound the inner light-ether so tightly to the physical body that we cannot perceive the real process which takes place when we remember. But, for any true spiritual knowledge, the light-ether within us has to be freed from this bondage so that the soul can feel itself outside the physical body in the light-ether of the world and beholding the inner light-ether. And the prayer quoted before was for souls who were striving to achieve this in the century following the Mystery of Golgotha.

The 'spawn of evil' mentioned in the prayer is Ahriman. 'Chaos' is the technical term for the experience of being outside the physical body. The 'higher place' is where the beings whose manifestation is the outer light, and the 'lower places' are where those behind the inner light-ether dwell. And the prayer asks for the overcoming of fear because it is through the power of fear that Ahriman seeks to prevent humans from knowing the light within. Both the prayer and Rudolf Steiner's commentary demonstrate how difficult it is for the modern mind to grasp the meaning of Gnostic texts such as the *Pistis Sophia*. What can any modern scholar make of the following passage in which Christ is quoted as saying:

> It came to pass, when I had come among the rulers of the aeons, that I looked down on the world of mankind and I found Elizabeth, the mother of John the Baptist, before she had conceived him. And I sowed into her a power which I had received from Iao the good, who is in the midst, so that the child she was to conceive would make proclamation before me and make ready my way and baptise with the water of the forgiveness of sins. Moreover, in place of the soul of the rulers which she was appointed to receive, I found the soul of the prophet Elijah in the aeons of the sphere and I took his soul and brought it to the Virgin of Light who gave it to her receivers and they cast it into the womb of Elizabeth.[3]

We know from the 'new Gnosis' that John was a reincarnation of Elijah. That this reincarnation was arranged by Christ and was not a simple matter, that it involved Iao (Yahweh), who rules over physical incarnation, is quite understandable for us.

But it can hardly make sense to mere scholarship.

Another Gnostic text is the *Acts of John*. These Acts purport to be a record by John the Disciple of what he experienced in the years he was with Jesus. The Acts contain the following passage:

> I will communicate to you those things whereof you are able to become hearers, that you may see the glory that surrounds him who was and is both now and for ever.
>
> For when he had chosen Peter and Andrew, who were brothers, he came to me and to my brother James, saying, 'I have need of you, come unto me.' And my brother said, 'John, this child on the shore who called us, what does he want?' And I said, 'What child?' He replied, 'The one who is beckoning to us.' And I answered, 'Because of our long watch we kept at sea you are not seeing straight, brother James: but do you not see the man who stands there, fair and comely and of a cheerful countenance?' But he said to me, 'Him I do not see, brother; but let us go and we shall see what it means.' And so when we had landed the ship, we saw him helping us to beach the ship.
>
> And when we left the place, wishing to follow him again, he again appeared to me, bald-headed but with a thick and flowing beard; but to James he appeared as a youth whose beard was just starting. We were perplexed, both of us, as to the meaning of what we had seen.[4]

What this strange passage conveys is the nature of Anthropos, the archetypal human being. The archetype of a plant manifests itself in the seed, the bud, the flower, the fruit; it is in all of them but is not identical with any of one these forms. In the same way Anthropos exists as childhood, adulthood, old age, all in one. This, as a spiritual experience, is what the passage describes. For the Gnostics, imbued with Neoplatonic philosophy, the idea or concept 'human being' was not an abstraction but a reality which necessarily included childhood, old age and the stages between. It was again on one of the twelve holy nights that Rudolf Steiner said about the Gnostics that the Gnosis wished to connect the ancient clairvoyant perception of the Sun Spirit who descended from divine spheres, with the understanding of the life of Christ Jesus on earth.

But it is striking to see how the human mind wanted to concentrate more and more on the contemplation of the merely earthly life of the Christ Jesus. It is striking to see how the simple human mind, which did not have the ancient clairvoyance to show the life of Jesus, was almost afraid of the grandiose idea of the Christ descending from the heavenly heights. The first Christians were fully unconscious of the ideas that Gnosis still possessed. They were afraid of these ideas.

Still into our time a certain fear is present with those who, although deeply touched by the Mystery of Golgotha, cannot pull themselves up to that recognition of the spirit ... However, what the Gnostics can still say about the heavenly Christ besides the earthly Christ is indeed very moving for us. And the gaze of our souls becomes in no way duller toward the earthly life of Christ Jesus if he is raised up now through new clairvoyance to the spiritual heights where the heavenly Christ is to be found and from where he has descended. Then it touches us so very deeply when the Gnosis relates:

> Jesus said:
> Look there, O Father,
> How this being on the Earth,
> Of all evil the goal and sacrifice,
> Far from thy breath wanders.
> Look, it flees bitter chaos,
> Helpless, how it should find its way through.
> Therefore, send me, O Father!
> Bearing the seal, I descend,
> I stride through the host of eons,
> Every holy teaching I unfold,
> Showing then the portrait of the gods.

And so I give you
Of the holy path
Deep-hidden lore:
'Gnosis' is its name for you.[5]

At the beginning of the century, when Rudolf Steiner became Secretary of the German section of the Theosophical Society, he also became editor and chief contributor of a periodical, *Lucifer-Gnosis*. The name was a tribute to the great spirits who had once sought to have not only faith, Pistis, but also wisdom, Sophia, in relation to the Mystery of Golgotha. Once this tradition was destroyed, it was inevitable that a split would come between knowledge and faith. Knowledge became thoroughly materialistic, and faith a belief in matters unknowable. In as far as anthroposophy wants to unite once again religion and science, it is a new Gnosis. And the poem quoted before could as well be spoken on behalf of anthroposophy. It is in a very real sense a Christmas poem, for it describes the descent of a spiritual being.

23

The Christian Mysteries

In his autobiography Rudolf Steiner speaks of the last years of the nineteenth century as a time in which it was his destiny to endure severe tests in his spiritual development. He writes: 'I was able to make progress during that period of testing only by contemplating, through spiritual perception, the evolution of Christianity. The insight I gained is described in *Christianity as Mystical Fact.*' Although the book was not published until 1902 it reflects this earlier period in Rudolf Steiner's life, a period of which he said in the same chapter: 'At that time, I had to rescue my spiritual worldview through inner storms.'[1]

One should not be deceived by the impersonal style in which *Christianity as Mystical Fact* is written into believing that the views expressed are the result of mere earnest study. What stands behind them is a titanic struggle of a kind which our superficial thinking can hardly imagine. And nowhere in the book is this struggle more perceptible than in the chapter which is intended to express the 'Essence of Christianity'.

We are first made to understand the difference and, because of it, the antagonism between the mystery tradition and Christianity. The mysteries taught people to seek the eternal spirit in themselves and to overcome the earthly personality, which was an obstacle on the path. Christianity saw the earthly personality as sanctified and redeemed through Christ's dwelling in the man Jesus, and in AD 869 made it a heresy to speak of the 'spirit' in a human being.

This problem also affected the Christian Gnostics. They had a profound understanding of the nature of the Christ who had descended from the highest realms of the spirit, but found it difficult to believe that such a being could unite itself and become one with the earthly personality, Jesus. Some Gnostics even maintained that the man people had seen in Palestine was only a phantom, an apparition, not a real human being of flesh and blood.

We can understand their difficulty by using an analogy with the archetypal plant in Goethe's sense. This is not any real plant but the universal pattern in accordance with which all plants grow. This universal principle of plant life is for us no more than an abstract concept. Goethe was a step nearer to the reality and saw it as an imagination. But in its own realm the plant archetype is a being as real as any human individuality. It will be clear that this plant archetype manifests itself in all plants but cannot be identified with any specific plant. Just because it is universal it cannot at the same time be specific. Imagine that someone would claim that in his garden there was a flower which was the archetypal plant. We would not be inclined to believe such a claim. For the Gnostics, Christ was a being of an infinitely higher order than the plant archetype, he was the Logos, the living wisdom from which all things have come – the universal pattern of all existence. How could a cosmic being of that order become a single human personality, the carpenter of Nazareth?

For us today the problems which worried the Gnostics may well seem absurd and not of a kind a modern person could take seriously. But strangely enough, Rudolf Steiner took them seriously; living with these problems was part of the inner battle mentioned before – the battle 'to rescue my spiritual worldview'. And when later he came to write this book and, in particular, the chapter on the essence of Christianity, he presented the problems of the Gnostics without providing the reader with an easy solution. In fact, towards the end of this chapter he takes the problem a step further by comparing the conception of God in the ancient mysteries with the God-idea developed by Christianity.

Someone on the path of the ancient mystery initiation was concerned with finding the divine within himself. He was in no doubt that the divine, as it exists in a human being, is not the divinity who created the world. And yet, something of the life of that ultimate God pulsed even in the divine spark that can be found in the human being. And this was sufficient for the ancient mysteries. They stayed with that which can be known and did not seek to penetrate to the God who is beyond human comprehension.

But this is the God of whom Christ said, 'I and the Father are one,' and 'No one can come to the Father except through me' (John 10:30, 14:6). It means that with the coming of Christ new mysteries begin and in these Christian mysteries the God who had been unknowable before can become knowable through Christ. The ancient mysteries spoke of the divine which the human soul can know through its own efforts, the Christian mysteries of a God we can only know through Christ. And this means that, on the Christian path, one could not begin without faith in the divinity of Christ.

As Rudolf Steiner points out in this connection, in the rift between the ancient mystery tradition and Christianity, another rift begins which persists to this day: the rift between knowledge and faith. No faith in the Christian sense was required from those who desired initiation in a mystery temple. It was understood that no educated Greek or Roman would believe in the literal truth of the mythologies on which popular religion was based. They looked upon the mythologies as symbols and the meaning of these symbols could be learned in the mysteries. But for the Christian the death and resurrection of the Christ Jesus is not a symbolic image. It is a reality in which he has to believe if he seeks to find the Christ.

This is something the Gnostics understood very well and it is nowadays well expressed in the title given to one of their holy books, the *Pistis Sophia*, which means faith-wisdom,

a wisdom or knowledge arising from faith. As mentioned
before, they looked upon this faith as coming from an inborn
sense of truth in the human being, but without this faith there
could be no Sophia. Rudolf Steiner draws attention to this
vital difference between the pre-Christian and the Christian
mysteries and adds that the Christian mystic is not without
preconceived notions *(voraussetztungslos)*.

One might regard it as a defect of the Christian mysteries
that he who seeks Christ has first to believe in him. But this lies
in the nature of Christ himself. We can understand this nature
if we realise the significance of the words he spoke when he
was brought before Pilate:

> Pilate said to him, 'So you are a king?' Jesus answered,
> 'You say that I am a king. For this end I was born, and
> for this I have come into the world, to bear witness to
> the truth. Every one who is of the truth hears my voice.'
> Pilate said to him, 'What is truth?' (John 18:37f).

Rudolf Steiner, speaking of this passage, points out that the
answer Christ gives to the question 'Are you a king?' Does not
make sense in the form we have in the text. What Christ really
said was: 'I am a king only if you say it from within yourself.'
What this passage is meant to convey is that Christ does not
impose his kingship or his divinity upon any human soul. The
soul must find in itself the recognition that Christ is lord of the
kingdom which is not of this world. This recognition is a *free
act*. If I were convinced by something outside myself, a miracle
performed before my eyes, historical documentary evidence,
or even the automatic processes of logic, it would not be in
my own freedom to accept Christ. Only in myself can I find
Aletheia, the truth that is part of the being Anthropos, the inner
truth which recognises Christ. This is what Christ meant when
he said: 'Every one that is of the truth hears my voice.'

It is because Christ leaves the human soul free that a free
act, that of faith, is necessary for the Christian mysteries.

It would be outside the scope of this book to discuss these Christian mysteries but, in fact, Rudolf Steiner had already done so and this is indicated by the last sentence of his chapter, which speaks of the difference between the Christian mystics of the Middle Ages and the mystics who had followed the path of the ancient mystery temples. This is followed by a footnote drawing attention to his book entitled *Mystics after Modernism*. It is a hint which should not be overlooked.

One of the personalities discussed in that book is the fourteenth-century mystic Johannes Tauler. And there is a quotation from his writings which happens to be the perfect answer to the problem that haunted the Gnostics: how the Logos could be incarnated in a single individuality. Tauler wrote:

> God accomplishes all his works in the soul and gives them to the soul, and the Father brings forth his only begotten Son in the soul as truly as he brings him forth in eternity, neither less nor more. What is brought forth when one says, 'God brings forth in the soul'? Is it a similitude of God, or is it an image of God, or is it something else of God? It is neither image nor similitude of God but the same God and the same Son whom the Father brings forth in eternity. It is nothing but the lovely divine Word, which is the other person in the Trinity. This does the Father bring forth in the soul.[2]

In these words lives the spirit of the Christian mysteries. And Tauler was specially prepared to express this spirit. He was already a well-known preacher when, after one of his sermons, he was approached by a layman who offered to instruct him in the mysteries of the divine. This layman is referred to as the Friend of God from the Highlands, but apart from this nothing else is known of him. Tauler followed that man and was transformed by what he learned.

Rudolf Steiner revealed that Zarathustra, who had left the body of Jesus at the baptism in the Jordan, later incarnated again and again and goes through the centuries as the guardian of esoteric Christianity.[3] He is known to those who have supersensible knowledge as Master Jesus, because he had been Jesus. And it was this Master Jesus who, as the Friend of God from the Highlands, instructed Johannes Tauler. This gives the Tauler's quoted words a special significance. They express the essence of Christianity.

24

Philo and Plotinus

In the lecture mentioned earlier in connection with the Gnosis of Valentinus, Rudolf Steiner draws attention to the height of human thought-life confined to the centuries immediately preceding and following the Mystery of Golgotha.[1] No period of human history either before or after that time has produced ideas as profound and subtle as those of the Greek and Roman Neoplatonic philosophers who lived around the time of the Mystery of Golgotha.

And – so said Rudolf Steiner – the clairvoyant who seeks to find the source of the spiritual light which shone for mankind at that time, cannot find the source in the physical world nor in the astral world and not even in the lower regions of devachan. Using, as he himself calls it, a 'symbolical' expression, Rudolf Steiner speaks of a 'star' that began to shine in the highest region of devachan in those centuries, a star three worlds removed from the world of the senses, and this is the source of the profound thought-light of that period.

No further explanation is given of the nature of this star but the reader is left with the impression that the light which shone from about 100 BC to AD 250 accompanied the Mystery of Golgotha and was in some way connected with it. It is a thought which can help to understand the two personalities, Philo and Plotinus, presented in the next chapter of *Christianity as Mystical Fact*, 'Christianity and Pagan Wisdom'. While the previous chapter emphasised the difference, and even opposition, between the pagan mystery wisdom and Christianity, we are now made aware how close they came in certain personalities. Both Philo and Plotinus expressed thoughts and speak of experiences we can recognise as Christian. Since neither of them had any direct contact with Christianity, they have to be regarded as souls illuminated by that star which shone from higher devachan, the sphere of intuition. Perhaps one is justified in calling this light the light of the Holy Spirit.

Philo of Alexandria was a Jew but, unlike the Jews of Palestine, an enthusiastic student of Greek thought, in particular of Neoplatonist philosophy. This form of Platonism contained a feature which derived from the mystery traditions: the interpretation of myths as images or symbols of inner soul experiences. The mythological battle between the Olympic gods and the Titans was, for the Neoplatonists, not something that had happened once in a distant past, but it was a struggle that took place in every human soul in which reason overcomes blind passions. Philo, the Hellenised Jew, applied the same method to the mythology of his own people and reinterpreted the Old Testament.

He took, for instance, the story of Exodus in the Old Testament and gave it a new meaning. The servitude of the Jews in Egypt stands for the soul's bondage to the physical body. Moses stands for the spiritual powers of the soul which can free it from that bondage. The Pharaoh who wants to keep the Israelites in Egypt is a symbol of our physical desires, which stand in the way of our spiritual striving. The crossing of the Red Sea is an image of crossing the threshold of the spiritual world. The years of wandering in the desert are a symbol of the loneliness the soul must endure before it can reach the Promised Land which is the conscious knowledge of one's immortal self.

Philo interprets even the story of creation in this manner. The soul which desires spiritual development must create in itself a division between that which is of a heavenly nature and that which is earthly. This corresponds to the words, 'In the beginning God created heaven and earth.' And then mankind's higher nature looks upon the earthly desires and passions and recognises their chaotic nature. This is the counterpart to the words of Genesis, 'And the earth was without form and void and darkness was upon the face of the deep. And the spirit of God moved upon the face of the waters.' But it is within the power of the human being to bring order into this inner force of chaos through the forms of self-discipline which have always been an integral part of spiritual development. The creation of this inner order is expressed in Genesis by the words, 'And God said, "Let there be light".'

It must not be assumed that drawing parallels of this kind between processes within the soul and the Old Testament was for Philo mere speculation, a play with thoughts, as it would be for a modern intellect. He spoke of matters that he had experienced intensively and profoundly. We have in Philo a man who had no connection with the esoteric stream within the Jewish religion. He was too far removed from these traditions, too much of a Greek in his thoughts and feelings, to have any common ground with pious rabbis or Essene communities. And the Pharisees would, without any doubt, have condemned his views as heretical and even blasphemous. But he had also no connection with the already decadent mystery cults of Greece or Egypt. The Jew in him would have found it abhorrent to enter a temple devoted to the worship of Isis or Demeter. His spiritual 'home' was the philosophy of Plato in the mystic form it had developed at that time. And so he entered upon a path of initiation on which he was only guided by his own intelligence and integrity. This is the reason why Rudolf Steiner can say of him:

> One might say that the temple in which Philo seeks
> initiation is simply and solely his own inward life
> and the higher experiences that come to him. With
> him, processes of a purely spiritual nature replace the
> initiatory ceremonies of the mysteries.

Philo was a contemporary of Jesus of Nazareth. In Palestine the Mystery of Golgotha took place and proclaimed to the world that initiation is no longer the preserve of the mystery temples; it is there for all souls who seek it. Philo knew nothing of these events but achieved in himself and through himself the stage of initiation which is called Illumination. Summarising Philo's achievement Rudolf Steiner writes:

> The God who poured himself into the world consummates his resurrection in the soul when his creative Word is understood in the soul and re-created there. Then man has given spiritual birth within himself to divinity, to the divine spirit that has become man, to the Logos, to Christ. In this sense, for Philo and those who thought as he did, the gaining of true knowledge was the birth of Christ within the world of spirit.[2]

These words have a striking resemblance to the words written by the medieval mystic Johannes Tauler and quoted in the previous chapter. Separated by more than a millennium – one a Jew with pagan culture, the other a devout Christian – they speak of the same mystic experience: the birth of the Logos, Christ, in the soul. This makes Philo of Alexandria remarkable. Even if one takes account of the special spiritual light, the 'star' that shone at that time, one is kept wondering about this Christian who was not a Christian.

On another occasion Rudolf Steiner said of Philo that he anticipated an attitude to the Roman Empire which became common among the early Christians: to hate what the Romans loved and to love what the Romans hated.[3] The Romans set great store by a person's family and ancestors. But Philo wrote, 'Pay no attention to whose descendant the body is. Consider only the descent of the soul' – a Christian view totally opposed to Roman thinking, and to much of present-day thinking too.

But Philo appears in quite a new light when one learns from a lecture given in 1903 that this individuality was reincarnated in the seventeenth century as the philosopher Spinoza and then again in the eighteenth century as the philosopher Fichte.[4] And it was of Fichte that the young Rudolf Steiner wrote to a friend that this philosopher's writings filled him with delight. He quoted from him a passage that begins with the words 'Life is love and the whole form and force of life consists of love and springs from love.' And Rudolf Steiner adds: 'He who understands something like this, not only with dead reason but as a living experience, has awakened to a special kind of life.'[5] The first dawn of this experience has to be seen in Fichte's incarnation as Philo of Alexandria.

Somebody who not only speaks of this experience but tries to describe it is the other personality of whom Rudolf Steiner wrote in this chapter of *Christianity as Mystical Fact,* the great Neoplatonist Plotinus. His evocation of a spiritual experience is quoted at length. Although the words of our earthly language are inadequate, one can at least feel the reality Plotinus tries to convey when he writes:

It has happened often.
  Roused into myself from my body – outside
everything else and inside myself – my gaze has met a
beauty wondrous and great. At such moments I have
been certain that mine was the better part, mine the best
of lives lived to the fullest, mine identity with the divine.[6]

The 'life' of which Plotinus speaks is not the life we experience in our body. It is a spiritual life outside the body. It is the life to which Christ referred when he said, 'I am the Way, the Truth and the Life.' The procedures of the mystery temples had enabled souls to come to this life, the life of the Logos, the life of the Word. But in the first centuries of the Christian era the life of the Word came into the world outside the mysteries, and individual souls such as Philo or Plotinus could find it through their own spiritual striving. The Christians came to it through their faith in the Christ Jesus.

There is a phenomenon which is characteristic of that period and which is intimately connected with this mystery of the life of the Word. Rudolf Steiner describes this phenomenon in a lecture as follows:

> Those pupils of the apostles who listened to the apostles could hear from the sound of their words something of the manner and the tonal quality of Christ Jesus's speech. This is something of immense significance. For it is particularly important to reflect on this sound, this quite distinctive quality of the way that Christ Jesus spoke if one is seeking to understand why those who heard him said that a special magical power resided in his words.[7]

We can see from this that the power of the living Word, of the life of the Word reverberated still in the apostles and was heard by those who listened to them. This life of the Word had come to philosophers who understood what was meant by the Logos; it came to the Christians who had faith in the words of Jesus Christ. Both these streams came together in John, the author of the gospel that proclaims, 'In the beginning was the Word.' There is no reason why a meeting of these two streams could not have taken place on a larger scale and why there could not have come into existence a church which combined Christianity with a knowledge and understanding of the principle of initiation. It did not happen – and the reason why the development of the Christian religion took a different direction forms the content of the last chapter of *Christianity as Mystical Fact*.

25

Saint Augustine

In a lecture of 1917 Rudolf Steiner speaks of certain things which have to be known if one wants to understand the development of Christianity in the early centuries following the Mystery of Golgotha. These things are also important for a deeper understanding of the last chapter of his book. In the course of this lecture Rudolf Steiner said:

> The essential quality of Roman history was that a human community was to be established which would more or less exclude man as a spiritual being. A society was to be brought into being where it would be meaningless to speak of man as a threefold being with a body, soul and spirit ...
>   At the court of justice where Christ Jesus was condemned, those referred to as the Sadducees played a leading part. What was their role when the Mystery of Golgotha took place? ... They were those who wanted to make everything deriving from the mysteries vanish away, disappear into oblivion. The Sadducees had a fear, a terror, an absolute dread of any form of mystery cult; but they were also the people wo had responsibility for the courts and likewise for the administration of Palestine. They were, however, wholly under the influence of the Roman state. Indeed they were the slaves of the Roman state.
> Another passage points out that this hatred of the spirit

and of the mystery traditions persisted even when Christianity
became the official Roman religion.

> In those circles where Christianity had become the
> official religion, there were increasing efforts to suppress
> the spirit, the very idea of the spirit. People felt that
> one should not make any reference to the spirit, for it
> was thought that this could lead to all the old ideas of a
> division of man into body, soul and spirit reviving once
> more.[1]

There are many passages of a similar content in the lectures
called *Building Stones to an Understanding of the Mystery of Golgotha*
and what they all convey is that the form which Christianity
took under Roman influence, inherited from pagan Rome
the hostility to the mysteries and the denial of the spirit in
man. It will be clear that this also meant the suppression of all
knowledge of the path of initiation.

If one accepts the main thesis of this book – that the
Mystery of Golgotha took place in order that eventually all
human souls should have the possibility of initiation, not just
a chosen few – then the Christianity which spread from Rome
throughout western Europe was from the beginning anti-
Christian. In the early centuries other forms of Christianity,
the various Gnostic churches, existed. Among the Gnostics
there existed much that came from mystery traditions. They
had profound concepts of man's spiritual nature. And for a
time these so-called heresies could hold out against the attacks
of the Roman Church.

This was the situation in the fourth century when Augustine
began his search for truth. He was brought up as a pagan and
so knew something of the mysteries. That is the reason why
he could write: 'What is now called the Christian religion
existed already among the ancients.' He had in his youth a
mystical experience and found in Plato and Plotinus concepts
to understand that experience. Having this kind of background

he was at first inclined towards a Gnostic form of Christianity, the Manicheans. It was the Manichean Bishop Faustus who made a strong impression on Augustine and whose teaching he followed. But then he turned against his teacher, rejected the Manichean and all other Gnostic doctrines and became a convert to the Church of Rome. He entered the priesthood and rose to the rank of bishop. Through his writings he became the most important of the Church Fathers, the men who formulated the ideas which gave Roman Christianity its philosophical justification.

What was it that made Augustine reject the Manichean doctrines? It was their appeal to the spirit in the human being, the spirit in himself. Faustus had told him to form his own judgement and not blindly to follow some authority. In contrast to this the Church of Rome demanded submission, obedience and unquestioning acceptance of its teaching. And Augustine found more comfort in obedience than in independence. The faith in Christ which is inherent in Christianity became for Augustine faith in the Church which claims to be Christ's representative on earth.

Augustine had made his choice, and because he was an outstanding personality, a mystic as well as an intellectual, a scholar and a gifted writer, his influence was far-reaching not only in his own time but also through centuries. To this day there are some intellectuals who, realising the emptiness of mere clever thought and despairing of coming to any truth through it, have found comfort in submission to the authority of the Catholic Church. The accusation made against a Manichean bishop – that his refusal to bow before the authority of the Church and to insist on following his own independent way was nothing but pride and arrogance – has been repeated, in one form or another, down the centuries whenever an individual diverges from the views of an entrenched authority.

In spite of the fact that Augustine had acknowledged that there had been Christianity in the ancient mysteries, it was he, more than any other individual, who ensured by submitting to Rome that European Christianity became ignorant of its connection with the mysteries and that all traces of this connection were obliterated. And as *Christianity as Mystical Fact* was written with the express purpose of re-establishing this connection, it can be regarded as a conscious attempt to undo what Augustine had done. No wonder that in the last chapter Rudolf Steiner devotes so much space to his great adversary.

But there remains a question. This Augustine really is an enigmatic personality. How could someone of his stature, someone with a deep understanding of the Neoplatonist philosophy, become a pillar of Roman Catholic dogmatism? With Philo of Alexandria we have found that his later incarnations illuminate what lived in this individuality at the time of the Mystery of Golgotha. With Augustine one can understand him better if one takes account of Rudolf Steiner's description of his previous incarnations.

The conquests of Alexander the Great resulted, as we have seen, in a civilisation in which the different mystery traditions of Persia, Egypt and Greece mixed and mingled, and in which these traditions were interpreted in the light of Greek philosophy. Hellenism spread over all the lands of the Mediterranean Sea, but there was one important exception: the Jews. It is true that at a later stage some Jews, like Philo of Alexandria, were drawn into the world of Hellenistic thought, but this would not have been possible two hundred years earlier. At that time the Jews of Palestine had come under the dominion of a Greek ruler who tried to force Hellenistic culture upon them. Statues of Greek gods were placed in the Temple at Jerusalem and religious customs that the Jews had practised for centuries were forbidden. The result was a rebellion led by a group of brothers, the Maccabees. The outstanding personality among them was the oldest brother, Judas. Under his leadership the rebellion succeeded and Palestine was freed from foreign dominion. However, Judas realised that his small country could not retain its independence for long, being surrounded by powerful neighbours. He therefore concluded a pact with Rome, which put Palestine under Roman protection.

It was a move which anticipated what the same individuality did as Augustine when he sought the spiritual protection of the Church of Rome. Judas the Maccabee had found that political independence was a condition fraught with uncertainties and dangers and he looked for safety under the shield of Rome. In the Augustine incarnation he felt the same way about spiritual matters. Here, too, independence could be dangerous and once again Rome offered a safe haven. But between Judas the Maccabee and Augustine there was another incarnation, more mysterious, more tragic than the other two lives. This individuality was the apostle known as Judas Iscariot.[2]

It is natural for anyone, even for somebody who is not a Christian, to feel horror and revulsion at the act of betrayal performed by this second Judas. Yet, as Rudolf Steiner points out, this betrayal was necessary, for without it the Mystery of Golgotha could not have taken place. It was a necessity that one soul should commit the worst sin in the history of mankind so that the salvation of mankind should be accomplished. Judas was this soul – and in this sense mankind is indebted to him.

And because what Judas did was necessary, his deed and the deeds of all who contributed to the passion of Christ, the soldiers, Pilot, the High Priest, were – as Rudolf Steiner said – without karma; there is no karmic retribution for anything they inflicted on Jesus Christ.[3]

And so Judas reincarnated as a personality who became a saint, the Church Father Augustine. If we consider, in the light of this knowledge, Augustine's decision to turn against the mystery wisdom, we can see that this too was a kind of betrayal – a betrayal of the true nature of Christianity as a 'mystical fact.' Yet this betrayal too was a necessity. The ancient wisdom had to die, had to be buried, so that it could arise in an entirely new form in the age of the consciousness soul.

Through this new mystery knowledge, anthroposophy, it is possible to understand the teaching of the ancient mysteries, the Christianity of the Gnostics, the religious philosophy of Philo and Plotinus – but anthroposophy is in no way a continuation or a renewal of any of these things. It is something new, born out of the spirit of our time. But like the ancient mystery knowledge, anthroposophy affirms that the human being is a spirit and that there is a path which leads us to a conscious realisation that we are spiritual beings and the descendants of higher beings. To show that this conviction lies also at the core of Christianity is the purpose of Rudolf Steiner's book, *Christianity as Mystical Fact*.

The Author

Charles Kovacs was born in Vienna on February 8, 1907. When he was still a young child the family moved to Nussdorf on the Danube, where the river flowed just before the house, so that he could see and hear the barges passing by, loading and unloading. Behind the house were forests of nut trees; to the left there shone a special light over the Kahlberg. It was here that he first went to school.

With the sudden death of his father, the family – his grandmother, mother and his younger brother Erwin – moved to their uncle's lovely villa in Baden at the foot of the Vienna Woods. At that time the inhabitants of Baden were forward-looking and had high civic standards. They built fine modern art galleries to show the new styles of painting that had become popular. Charles was very interested in painting. He visited these galleries and then worked on his own pictures when he went home. He was about twelve years old when he showed his paintings to his respected art teacher, Professor Friedrich Thetter. Thetter's two children were also Charles' friends at the school and Charles was invited to come regularly and to bring his paintings. Professor Thetter, a long-standing anthroposophist, then introduced Charles to the fundamentals of art, to Goethe, then to Rudolf Steiner and anthroposophy. It was an encounter Charles never forgot. He was deeply grateful to Professor Thetter and they remained close friends, corresponding even when they were far apart. Charles and his brother Erwin both became members of the Anthroposophical Society, Charles when he was 22 years old.

Life was lively in Vienna. Charles would listen to the latest hits on the wireless in the evenings and next day he would play them to his friends, for both brothers had learned from their mother to play the piano. His uncle employed him for a time in his warehouse, selling coffee and tea, and it was his son who later, when Charles was 32, invited him out to Kenya. He enjoyed working on a large farm; the compound was so extensive that he needed a horse to get around it all and for a while he was in charge of a sawmill. It was during that time that he drew (on the backs of reference cards used at the mill) and compiled a small book of Pietas – each drawing so different!

Then came the Second World War and he volunteered to join the British Army. He was proud to be able to say that he fought with the 8th Army at El Alamein. His army discharge paper says of him: 'This man is thoroughly trustworthy, outstanding for his intelligence and linguistic ability. Speaks English and German fluently and has a fair knowledge of French. Extremely energetic and untiring in his work. Capable of organization and control of staff. Has responded to calls of duty beyond the normal requirements.'

After the war he returned briefly to Kenya where he had started an anthroposophical study group. In April 1948 Charles came to London. A relative needed somebody to take on the responsibility of his firm in Golden Square, Piccadilly, and Charles worked there for about eight years. It was well-paid work, but it was a heavy burden. Before long he came to the anthroposophical group meeting one Monday evening; this was where we met, and within six months we married. Charles was soon asked to take over the study group at Museum Street and as part of his work for this group he translated works by Rudolf Steiner not then available in English. He became a member of the Council of the Anthroposophical Society and gave many lectures. Our home was, as Charles wanted, frequented by members of the group most evenings. When they had left he would often paint or draw, an activity which for him seemed a necessity. It was a member of the group who urged Charles to become a teacher. And so it came about that we came to Edinburgh in 1956 to teach at the Rudolf Steiner School.

Then his most productive years began. He took over a Class 4 of thirty-five children. As part of his preparation, he wrote out his lessons day by day so that he built into his teaching a structure, inspired by Rudolf Steiner's curriculum, which could satisfy the growing child. These notes now stand as a fine example of the new and living way Steiner wanted his curriculum presented to children. Some of the notes have been made into books and they have been widely used in many different schools.

As a Waldorf teacher, Charles' creative talents were called on more than ever before. His special gift for painting and drawing was put to good use and his work was much in evidence around the school. For example the kindergarten, which I took over, was blessed and looked upon by the guardian angel that Charles painted. He composed songs and poems, he wrote plays for his classes; Charles was completely given over to his teaching. At the same time he held parents' evenings, had regular study groups and gave lectures within the Anthroposophical Society and to the public. For a time he travelled regularly to Ilkeston in Derbyshire to work with a group of friends there. His pupils wanted him to come to the upper school to give them the philosophy main lesson when he had already retired.

Charles was about 82 when he found that his right leg, injured during the war, was getting more troublesome; until then he regularly gave study groups and lectures outside the home but gradually he found that walking had become difficult. Now he studied even more intensively with the groups and people who met here regularly, working on fundamental books by Rudolf Steiner. In between he found time to paint, but he never put his signature to any of his creative work.

Charles died in 2001. He gave me so much, I would like to thank him.

Dora Kovacs

From Charles Kovacs, *The Spiritual Background to Christian Festivals,* Floris Books 2007.

References

1 The Secrecy of the Mysteries
1   See, for instance, Steiner, *The Mysteries of the East and of Christianity,* lecture of Feb 3, 1913.
2   See Steiner, *The Gospel of St John,* lecture of May 25, 1908.
3   *Leonardo da Vinci,* lecture of Feb 13, 1913.

2 Mystery Knowledge and Popular Religion
1   Letter to Richard Specht of Nov 30, 1890, *Briefe II 1890– 1925,* p. 37 (quoting from opening pages of Fichte's *The Way to the Blessed Life).*

3 Mystery Knowledge and Early Philosophy
1   See, for instance, *Old and New Methods of Initiation,* lecture of Jan 1, 1922.
2   *Mystery Knowledge and Mystery Centres,* lecture of Dec 2, 1923.

4 The Awakening of Thinking in Greece
1   For instance, *The Foundations of Esotericism,* lecture of Sep 28, 1905.
2   *Christianity as Mystical Fact,* chapter 'Plato as a Mystic', p. 58.
3   *The Philosophy of Freedom,* addition to Chapter 8, p. 119.

5 The Interpretation of Ancient Myths
1   *The Inner Nature of Man,* lecture of April 11, 1914, pp. 102f.

6 A Buddhist Fable and the Myth of Osiris
1   *Anthroposophical Leading Thoughts,* letter of Nov 17, 1924, p. 13.

7 The Myth of Heracles
1 *Education for Special Needs,* lecture of June 27, 1924.
2 *The Ten Commandments,* lecture of Dec 14, 1908.

9 Odysseus
1 *Apocalypse of John,* lecture of July 21, 1908.

10 The Myth of Demeter and Persephone
1 *The Temple Legend,* lecture of Oct 7, 1904, pp. 44, 46.
2 *Egyptian Myths and Mysteries,* lecture of Sep 12, 1908, p. 118.
3 *The Festivals and Their Meaning,* 'On the Three Magi', lecture of Dec 30, 1904, pp. 89f.
4 *Egyptian Myths and Mysteries,* lecture of Sep 12, 1908, p. 119.

11 The Egyptian Mysteries
1 *The Principle of Spiritual Economy,* lecture of May 31, 1909.
2 Compare published translations *Christianity as Mystical Fact,* p. 84 of 1972 British edition or p. 88 of 2008 American edition.
3 Psalm 82:6, John 10:34.

13 Events in the Gospels
1 *The Fifth Gospel,* lecture of Oct 5, 1913.

14 The Awakening of Lazarus
1 *The World of the Senses and the World of the Spirit,* lecture of Dec 28, 1911.
2 *Building Stones for an Understanding of the Mystery of Golgotha,* lecture of April 14, 1917.

15 The Initiation of Mankind
1 *Esoteric Lessons 1904–1909,* April 15, 1909.
2 For instance, *Problems of Society,* lecture of Sep 12, 1919.
3 *Cosmic and Human Metamorphoses,* lecture of Feb 6, 1917.

16 The Four Riders of the Apocalypse
1 *Awake! For the Sake of the Future,* lecture of Jan 27, 1923, pp. 146f.

17 The Fifth, Sixth and Seventh Seals
1 *Good and Evil Spirits,* lecture of May 13, 1908, p. 123.
2 *Mysteries of the Sun,* lecture of Aug 25, 1918.

19 The Time of Jesus

1   *According to Matthew,* lecture of Sep 5, 1910.
2   *Esoteric Lessons 1910–1912,* lecture of Sep 1, 1912.
3   *According to Matthew,* lecture of Sep 10, 1910.
4   *Spiritual Science as a Foundation for Social Forms,* lecture of Aug 7, 1920. See also Prokofieff, *The Spiritual Origins of Eastern Europe,* pp. 225f.

21 The Gnostics

1   *Christ and the Spiritual World,* lecture of Dec 28, 1913.
2   *The Inner Nature of Man,* lecture of April 10, 1914, p. 80.

22 The *Pistis Sophia* and the *Acts of John*

1   *Unifying Humanity Spiritually,* lecture of Jan 2, 1916, p. 103.
2   *Unifying Humanity Spiritually,* lecture of Jan 2, 1916, p. 104.
3   Mead, *First Book of the Pistis Sophia,* Chapter 7.
4   *Acts of John* 88–89. From Elliott, *The Apocryphal New Testament.*
5   *Inner Reading and Inner Hearing,* lecture of Dec 26, 1914, pp. 156f.

23 The Christian Mysteries

1   *Autobiography,* Chapter 57, pp. 238f (Chapter 26 in *Course of my Life* edition).
2   Quoted in *Mystics of the Renaissance,* pp. 53f. From Tauler, *Sermons* (Sermon 83).
3   *According to Luke,* lecture of Sep 21, 1909.

24 Philo and Plotinus

1   *Christ and the Spiritual World,* lecture of Dec 28, 1913.
2   *Christianity as Mystical Fact,* pp. 137, 140.
3   *Building Stones for an Understanding of the Mystery of Golgotha,* lecture of April 17, 1917, pp. 172f.
4   *Über die Astrale Welt und das Devachan,* lecture of Aug 24, 1903, also *Our Connection with the Elemental World,* lecture of June 5, 1913.
5   Letter to Richard Specht of Nov 30, 1890, *Briefe II 1890–1925,* p. 37.
6   Plotinus, *Enneads* IV, 8, 1.
7   *Building Stones,* lecture of April 10, 1917, pp. 172f.

25 Saint Augustine

1   *Building Stones,* lecture of March 27, 1917, pp. 133f, 138f.
2   *The Gospel of St Mark,* lecture of Sep 16, 1912. See also Pelikan, *Lebensbegegnung mit Leonardos Abendmal.*
3   *The Fifth Gospel,* lecture of Oct 3, 1913.

Bibliography

Elliott, J.K. *The Apocryphal New Testament,* Oxford University Press 1993.

Fichte, J.G. *The Way Towards the Blessed Life,* (Tr. William Smith) 1849, reprinted Leopold Classic Library, USA 2016.

James, M.R. *The Apocryphal New Testament,* Oxford University Press 1924.

Mead, G.R.S. *The First Book of the Pistis Sophia,* Kessinger, USA 2010.

Pelikan, W. *Lebensbegegnung mit Leonardos Abendmal,* Verlag am Goetheanum, Dornach 1988.

Prokofieff, Sergei O. *The Spiritual Origins of Eastern Europe and the Future Mysteries of the Holy Grail,* Temple Lodge Press, UK 1993.

Steiner, Rudolf. Volume Nos refer to the Collected Works (CW), or to the German Gesamtausgabe (GA).

—, *According to Luke* (CW 114) SteinerBooks, USA 2001.

—, *According to Matthew* (CW 123) SteinerBooks, USA 2002.

—, *Anthroposophical Leading Thoughts* (CW 26) Rudolf Steiner Press, UK 1973.

—, *Apocalypse of John* (CW 104) Anthroposophic Press, USA 1985.

—, *Autobiography: Chapters in the Course of My Life* (CW 28) SteinerBooks, USA 2000 (previously published as *The Course of My Life,* Anthroposophic Press, USA 1951).

—, *Awake! For the Sake of the Future* (CW 220) SteinerBooks, USA 2014.

—, *Briefe II 1890–1925* (GA 39) Rudolf Steiner Verlag, Dornach 1987.

—, *Building Stones for an Understanding of the Mystery of Golgotha* (CW 175) Rudolf Steiner Press, UK 2015.

—, *Christ and the Spiritual World* (CW 149) Rudolf Steiner Press, UK 2008.

—, *Christianity as Mystical Fact* (1902, CW 8) Rudolf Steiner Press, UK 1972 (a freer translation also published by SteinerBooks, USA 2008).

—, *Cosmic and Human Metamorphoses* (part of CW 175) SteinerBooks, USA 2015.

—, *Education for Special Needs: The Curative Education Course* (CW 317) Rudolf Steiner Press, UK 2014.

—, *Egyptian Myths and Mysteries* (CW 106) Anthroposophic Press, USA 1971.

—, *Esoteric Lessons 1904–1909* (CW 266/1) SteinerBooks, USA 2007.

—, *Esoteric Lessons 1910–1912* (CW 266/2) SteinerBooks, USA 2012.

—, *The Festivals and Their Meaning*, Rudolf Steiner Press, UK 1996.

—, *The Fifth Gospel* (CW 148) Rudolf Steiner Press, UK 1985.

—, *The Foundations of Esotericism* (CW 93a) Rudolf Steiner Press, UK 1983.

—, *Good and Evil Spirits and their Influence on Humanity* (CW 102) Rudolf Steiner Press, UK 2014.

—, *The Gospel of St John* (CW 103) Anthroposophic Press, USA 1984.

—, *The Gospel of St Mark* (CW 139) Anthroposophic Press, USA 1990.

—, *The Inner Nature of Man and Our Life Between Death and Rebirth* (CW 153) Rudolf Steiner Press, UK 2013.

—, *Inner Reading and Inner Hearing* (GA 156) SteinerBooks, USA 2008.

—, *Knowledge of Higher Worlds: How Is It Achieved?* Rudolf Steiner Press, UK 2009 (also published as *How to Know Higher Worlds: A Modern Path of Initiation*, Anthroposophic Press, USA 1994.)

—, *Leonardo da Vinci: His Spiritual and Intellectual Greatness at the Turning Point of the New Age*, typescript at wn.rsarchive.org/Lectures/19130213p01.html

—, *Harmony of the Creative Word* (CW 230) Rudolf Steiner Press, UK 2002.

—, *The Mysteries of the East and of Christianity* (CW 144) Rudolf Steiner Press, UK 1972.

—, *Mysteries of the Sun and of the Threefold Man*, typescript at wn.rsarchive.org/Lectures/GA183/English/LRZ254/MysSun_index.html

—, *Mystery Knowledge and Mystery Centres* (CW 232) Rudolf Steiner Press, UK 1997.

—, *Mystics after Modernism: Discovering the Seeds of a New Science in the Renaissance* (CW 7) SteinerBooks, USA 2000.

—, *Old and New Methods of Initiation* (CW 210) Rudolf Steiner Press, UK 1991.

—, *Our Connection with the Elemental World* (GA 158) Rudolf Steiner Press, UK 2017.

—, *An Outline of Esoteric Science* (CW 13) Anthroposophic Press, USA 1991.

—, *The Philosophy of Freedom* (CW 4) Rudolf Steiner Press, UK 1964.

—, *The Principle of Spiritual Economy* (CW 109) Anthroposophic Press, USA 1986.

—, *Problems of Society: An Esoteric View, from Lucifer Past to Ahrimanic Future* (CW 193) Rudolf Steiner Press, UK 2016.

—, *The Spiritual Hierarchies and the Physical World* (CW 110) SteinerBooks, USA 2008.

—, *Spiritual Science as a Foundation for Social Forms* (CW 199) Anthroposophic Press, USA 1986.

—, *The Temple Legend* (CW 93) Rudolf Steiner Press, UK 2000.

—, *The Ten Commandments,* Anthroposophic Press, USA 1978.

—, *Über die astrale Welt und das Devachan* (GA 88) Rudolf Steiner Verlag, Dornach 1999.

—, *Unifying Humanity Spiritually Through the Christ Impulse* (CW 165) Rudolf Steiner Press, UK 2014.

—, *The World of the Senses and the World of the Spirit* (CW 134) Rudolf Steiner Press, UK 2014.

Tauler, Johannes, *Sermons,* Paulist Press, New York 1979.

Index

Other Books by Charles Kovacs

General interest
> The Apocalypse in Rudolf Steiner's Lecture Series
> The Spiritual Background to Christian Festivals

Classes 4 and 5 (age 9–11)
> The Human Being and the Animal World

Classes 5 and 6 (age 10–12)
> Ancient Greece
> Botany

Class 6 (age 11–12)
> Ancient Rome

Classes 6 and 7 (age 11–13)
> Geology and Astronomy

Class 7 (age 12–13)
> The Age of Discovery

Classes 7 and 8 (age 12–14)
> Muscles and Bones

Class 8 (age 13–14)
> The Age of Revolution

Class 11 (age 16–17)
> Parsifal and the Search for the Grail

Also by Charles Kovacs

The Apocalypse in Rudolf Steiner's Lecture Series

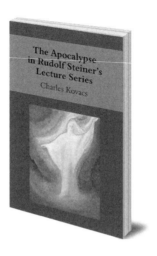

In 1908, Rudolf Steiner gave a series of lectures about the Book of Revelation. He showed that the messages to the seven churches and the unsealing of the seven seals should be understood as references to initiation. In this light, the great images of the Apocalypse take on new meaning.

As well as being a Steiner-Waldorf class teacher, Charles Kovacs was much in demand as an experienced and insightful lecturer for adults. In this book, he helps us make sense of the apocalyptic imagery, including the four beasts, the four riders, the woman clothed with the sun, and the New Jerusalem.

The book is illustrated with Kovacs' own colour paintings.

florisbooks.co.uk

The Spiritual Background to Christian Festivals

The rhythms of the earth can be seen in, for example, the daily cycle of day and night, or in the changing seasons. Rudolf Steiner spoke about how Christian festivals such as Easter, Whitsun and Christmas fitted not just into these patterns, but also into larger cosmic rhythms and, on a smaller scale, human rhythms.

In this concise, readable book Charles Kovacs explores the structure of our calendar year and looks in detail at the background to each Christian festival, including lesser-known ones such as St John's Tide and Michaelmas.

This book is based on lectures Charles Kovacs originally gave at the Rudolf Steiner School in Edinburgh.

florisbooks.co.uk

Floris Books

For news on all our **latest books,**
and to receive **exclusive discounts,**
join our mailing list at:

florisbooks.co.uk

Plus subscribers get a FREE book
with every online order!